4/05
1 6/07(13/07)

Joseph Stalin

Other books in the Heroes and Villains series include:

Heroes and Villains

Joseph Stalin

James Barter

B STALIN, J. BAR
Barter, James
Josef Stalin

$28.70
CENTRAL   31994012285471

LUCENT BOOKS
An imprint of Thomson Gale, a part of The Thomson Corporation

THOMSON

GALE

Detroit • New York • San Francisco • San Diego • New Haven, Conn. • Waterville, Maine • London • Munich

LIBRARY OF CONGRESS CATALOGING-IN-PUBLICATION DATA

Barter, James, 1946–
  Joseph Stalin / by James Barter.
    p. cm. — (Heroes and villains)
Includes bibliographical references and index.
ISBN 1-59018-557-9 (hardcover : alk. paper)
1. Stalin, Joseph, 1879–1953. 2. Heads of state—Soviet Union—Biography. 3. Soviet Union—History—1925–1953. I. Title. II. Series.
DK268.S8B275 2005
947.084'2'092—dc22
                                                                2004022545

Printed in the United States of America

Contents

Foreword

Good and evil are an ever-present feature of human history. Their presence is reflected through the ages in tales of great heroism and extraordinary villainy. Such tales provide insight into human nature, whether they involve two people or two thousand, for the essence of heroism and villainy is found in deeds rather than in numbers. It is the deeds that pique our interest and lead us to wonder what prompts a man or woman to perform such acts.

Samuel Johnson, the eminent eighteenth-century English writer, once wrote, "The two great movers of the human mind are the desire for good, and fear of evil." The pairing of desire and fear, possibly two of the strongest human emotions, helps explain the intense fascination people have with all things good and evil—and, by extension, heroic and villainous.

People are attracted to the person who reaches into a raging river to pull a child from what could have been a watery grave for both, and to the person who risks his or her own life to shepherd hundreds of desperate black slaves to safety on the Underground Railroad. We wonder what qualities these heroes possess that enable them to act against self-interest, and even their own survival. We also wonder if, under similar circumstances, we would behave as they do.

Evil, on the other hand, horrifies as well as intrigues us. Few people can look upon the drifter who mutilates and kills a neighbor or the dictator who presides over the torture and murder of thousands of his own citizens without feeling a sense of revulsion. And yet, as Joseph Conrad writes, we experience "the fascination of the abomination." How else to explain the overwhelming success of a book such as Truman Capote's *In Cold Blood*, which examines in horrifying detail a vicious and senseless murder that took place in the American heartland in the 1960s? The popularity of murder mysteries and Court TV is also evidence of the human fascination with villainy.

Most people recoil in the face of such evil. Yet most feel a deep-seated curiosity about the kind of person who could commit a terrible act. It is perhaps a reflection of our innermost fears that we wonder whether we could resist or stand up to such behavior in our presence or even if we ourselves possess the capacity to commit such terrible crimes.

The Lucent Books Heroes and Villains series capitalizes on our fascination with the perpetrators of both good and evil by introducing readers to some of history's most revered heroes and hated villains. These include heroes such as Frederick Douglass, who knew firsthand the humiliation of slavery and, at great risk to himself, publicly fought to abolish the institution of slavery in America. It also includes villains such as Adolf Hitler, who is remembered both for the devastation of Europe and for the murder of 6 million Jews and thousands of Gypsies, Slavs, and others whom Hitler deemed unworthy of life.

Each book in the Heroes and Villains series examines the life story of a hero or villain from history. Generous use of primary and secondary source quotations gives readers eyewitness views of the life and times of each individual as well as enlivens the narrative. Notes and annotated bibliographies provide stepping-stones to further research.

JOSEPH STALIN: THE ENIGMA

Barely a handful of historical periods can match the moral corruption and unrestrained brutality of the reign of Joseph Stalin, leader of the Soviet Union from 1924 until 1953. Still to this day, the name Stalin conjures an image of a frightening figure who was cold and calculating. Although rarely mixing with the public, Stalin's paranoid suspicion of his own colleagues, military, and public prompted him to unleash a vast network of secret police to spy on them in a never-ending search to eliminate anyone who might criticize or conspire against him. This policy led to a culture of terror, betrayal, and the extermination of millions of innocent people. By all respected accounts, Stalin is ranked as one of the most repressive tyrants in history.

For almost two decades Stalin worked to create an illusion of greatness that he presented to the outside world. He boasted that he had established a viable economy for his nation, defended his people against enemy aggression with great effectiveness, and took the Soviet Union from a second-rate nation to one of the most advanced in the world. All success, he triumphantly proclaimed, was the result of his leadership and economic ideology of communism. All of the failures were the fault of others.

Yet those living inside Stalin's tyrannical dictatorship knew a very different story. For tens of millions of people, Stalin's long autocratic rule was characterized by fear. He inflicted reccurring waves of terror, each on a grander scale than the previous one. Anyone suspected of criticizing Stalin or of failing to support his decisions with unflagging loyalty might expect a knock at the door in the dead of night from the secret police. Entire families were often pulled from their homes, arrested, tortured, and shot. It is now estimated by historians that the death toll under Stalin was certainly in excess of 20 million people and may reach 30 million once all secret Soviet documents are released. Historian Nikolai Tolstoy describes how Stalin maintained this atmosphere of control: "Stalin's great achievement was to place the entire population of nearly two hundred million people wholly in the power of the police, while himself retaining in turn absolute power over the police."[1]

Stalin's cruelty is well documented, but little else is known about the man. His personal life, private thoughts, and motivations for inflicting such suffering remain largely unknown. He remains more of an enigma than any other twentieth-century world leader. British prime minister Sir Winston Churchill once characterized Stalin's unpredictable personality as "a riddle, wrapped in a mystery, inside an enigma."[2] Historian Bertram Wolfe, in his work on the Russian Revolution, *Three Who Made a Revolution*, agreed with Churchill's characterization, adding, "So silently did

A guard tower and the remains of a barrack at a Soviet death camp in Siberia stand as mute testimony to the horrors many Soviet citizens endured under Joseph Stalin's dictatorial rule.

[Stalin] rise to power that he seemed hardly to have attracted the attention of his contemporaries until he was already in the Kremlin. . . . We [historians] are beset with obscurities and contradictions at every step."[3]

One of the difficulties of understanding this enigmatic man, which adds to his mystery, is the lack of solid documentation recording his reign. Stalin meticulously destroyed personal letters, private notes, telephone logs, and formal archives in order to obscure the terror he committed and to maintain his cloak of secrecy. Furthermore, unlike most world leaders of his time who lived to old age, Stalin never wrote an autobiography. It is for these reasons that contemporary historians struggle to explain Stalin's rise to power and dominance over his nation of 200 million people, as well as much of Europe, with seemingly little resistance from within or outside. This lack of historical records is highlighted by Russian historian Edvard Radzinsky, who writes:

He had succeeded in plunging the story of his life and the whole history of his country into impenetrable darkness. Systematically destroying his comrades in arms, he at once obliterated every trace of them in history. He personally directed the constant and relentless purging of the archives. He surrounded with the deepest secrecy everything even remotely relevant to the sources of his power. He converted the archives into closely guarded fortresses.[4]

Difficult as it may be to understand Stalin's elusive personality and political strategies, it is important to attempt to untangle them. Although Stalin has been discredited as one of the most reviled autocrats because of his repressive rule, there is still much to be learned about his place in European history and how he orchestrated his rise to power.

Chapter One

MODEST BEGINNINGS

Iosif Vissarionovich Dzhugashvili, who thirty-four years later would take the name Joseph Stalin, was born on December 21, 1879. He grew up in the city of Gori in the heart of the rural Soviet republic of Georgia. His childhood was marked by poverty, family violence, the death of three siblings, and the early loss of his father. As a young man, Stalin engaged in youthful rebellion and

Georgia

Caucasus

RUSSIA

Mountains

• Sukhumi

Kutaisi •

Black Sea

GEORGIA

• Batumi

Gori

⭐ Tbilisi

TURKEY

ARMENIA

AZERBAIJAN

Born into a life of poverty, Joseph Stalin grew up in this shack in the rural Soviet republic of Georgia.

displayed a ruthless temperament that would later define his behavior as the most horrific leader who ever ruled the Soviet Union.

Growing Up in Gori

Unique among Soviet republics, Georgia rests on the eastern shores of the Black Sea and extends inland to the east.

Framed on the north by the Caucasus Mountains, Georgia prospered from a network of cascading rivers flowing from snowcapped peaks, which provided lush crops for peasant farmers, thick growths of timber for loggers, and green meadows for ranchers pasturing cattle. Such an ideal coastal location filled its fish markets with a wealth of species for the young Joseph Stalin, who preferred the nickname Soso, meaning "Little Joey."

Relatively little is known about Stalin's family. They lived in a tilting two-story shack made of mismatched pieces of lumber with just two small windows providing the only interior light. The floor was made of crushed brick, which absorbed the rain that dripped through the roof. The poverty of the Dzhugashvili family was tragically accompanied by death. Joseph was the youngest of four siblings and the only one to live long enough to attend elementary school. His father was Vissarion Ivanovich Dzhugashvili, a struggling village shoemaker. There remains some question as to whether Vissarion was the boy's biological father because Stalin once confided in a private conversation that his father had been a priest. Whatever the truth might be, Vissarion, known to Stalin as Beso, was an alcoholic whose excessive drinking led to regular beatings of Joseph and his mother, Ekaterina Gheladze Dzhugashvili, whose nickname was Keke.

Beso and Keke

Joseph Stalin grew up in a poor and abusive family. Neither his father nor his mother ever received an education. Apparently neither could read nor write, and neither spoke any language other than their native Georgian, which was different from the dominant Russian language. When he was employed, Beso worked as a low-wage shoemaker in a boot factory in the city of Tiflis (modern Tbilisi), the capital of the Georgian republic. To supplement her husband's meager income, Keke worked hard at the traditional menial jobs of a washerwoman, taking in laundry and sewing for neighbors and scrubbing floors in nearby schools and hospitals.

Stalin rarely spoke of his father, but when he did it was in loathsome tones. Beso's harsh and unforgiving temper when he was sober gave way to physical violence and mental abuse directed at the young boy and his mother following heavy bouts of drinking. Historian Ronald Hingley, in his book *Joseph Stalin: Man and Legend*, sees a possible cause and effect between the beatings laid on Stalin as a boy and his later ruthless behavior as a dictator: "He [Beso] would thrash the infant Joseph, whom these terrible undeserved beatings rendered as tough and ruthless as the brute who administered them."[5] On one occasion, Joseph threw a knife at his father, prompting Keke to hide her son at a neighbor's house until calm could be restored.

When Joseph was seven, Beso took him to work at the boot factory as an apprentice. Records at the factory indicate that his apprenticeship did not last long. Joseph hated the job—and his father's constant criticism—and wanted to come home. Keke supported his desire to return because she wanted him to get an education and become a priest. With his mother's support, Joseph quit the

Keke

Joseph Stalin's mother, Keke, exerted more influence over Stalin as a boy than any other person. As a devoted mother she took sole responsibility for his education and value system of hard work and personal sacrifice. Because Joseph was the only of her four children to survive childhood, the two remained close until Stalin was expelled from the seminary and began his radical revolutionary activities.

Following his expulsion, Stalin did not see his mother again until he had risen to power in the Bolshevik Party after the Russian Revolution. At that time, Stalin uprooted Keke from her humble home in Gori and moved her to an opulent palace that had belonged to one of the czar's personal friends in Tiflis. Since Keke was nearing seventy at the time and had lived her entire life in terrible poverty, she could not adjust to a life of luxury in a palace. Instead, Keke confined herself to a single bedroom, cooked her own food, cleaned her own clothes, and continually asked her son for a more modest home, a request he regularly denied.

While Stalin ruled the nation, the two visited only twice. He invited his mother to Moscow on several occasions, but she refused because of her discomfort in large cities. Stalin refused to travel to Tiflis or anywhere else, because of his fear of assassination. In

spite of their separation, the two exchanged many short letters in which Keke regularly told her son that she was not impressed with his fame and power and that he would have done better if he had become a priest. Nonetheless, Stalin saw to it that Keke was well cared for. However, when she died, Stalin asked a friend to make the funeral arrangements and then refused to attend the services. Many were shocked by what they perceived to be his callous refusal to publicly recognize his mother's death.

Throughout her life, Stalin's mother, Keke, remained convinced that her son should have entered the priesthood.

As a young student at the Gori Church School, Stalin often got into fistfights with his classmates.

tedious low-paying job and returned home, where he took comfort with her. Furious about the situation, Beso threatened Keke, "Want your son to become a bishop, do you? You'll never live to see it. I'm a cobbler and that is what he will be."[6]

Beso's inflexible and offensive attitude did not deter Keke. In 1888 Keke's dream came true when she finalized arrangements for Joseph to be educated and trained for the priesthood at the local elementary school, the Gori Church School. To increase her income to pay the small tuition, Keke cleaned the homes of her son's teachers.

Elementary School

Keke scraped together enough money to enroll Joseph in the Gori elementary school for boys, an experience Joseph found miserable. The initial weeks at the seminary were tough for the young boy. He was immediately punished for fighting and earned an early reputation as a quick-tempered troublemaker. It was also at this time that Joseph was forced to give up the Georgian language in favor of the more prevalent Russian language. Although he learned Russian, he was never able to shake off his Georgian accent and suffered merciless taunts from the other boys. Such taunts were cause for fistfights and outbursts of anger. Those who knew Joseph at this time recall that one of his few happy moments during his initial stay at the school was receiving the news that his father had been beaten to death in a drunken brawl.

More taunts were soon to follow. During his first years at the elementary school, Joseph suffered terribly from several physical abnormalities. He was very short for his age; the few photographs of his seminary class show him to be the shortest boy in the class. Even at maturity he was only five feet four inches, and for the rest of his life his shortness rankled him, causing him to wear platform shoes and other devices in an effort to appear taller than he actually was. When Joseph was nine years old, smallpox spread through the school population, leaving his face badly scarred and pitted for the rest of his life. Viciously mocked when he returned to school, classmates labeled him "Pocky." Then, a case of blood poisoning caused his left arm to slightly wither and grow shorter than his right, giving him a somewhat misshapen, lopsided appearance. Later in life Stalin's many afflictions prompted the Russian novelist Boris Pasternak to describe him as "a man looking like a crab. The whole of his face was yellow and it was pitted all over with pockmarks. He was dwarfish—disproportionately broad and no taller than a twelve year old boy, but with an odd looking face."[7]

Pockmarked, disfigured, and short, Joseph responded to the childhood taunts and mockery with his fists, establishing a reputation for cruelty. The qualities of aggression and cunning that would later mark his rise to power were first evidenced in this school. One day on the school grounds, when Joseph was ten or eleven, another boy insulted him and a fight ensued. The two fought on an equal footing until Joseph's adversary quit when the bell rang, signaling a return to class. Assuming the fight was over, the boy turned his back on Joseph and began walking away when, without warning, Joseph savagely attacked from behind, threw the boy to the ground, and triumphantly planted his knee in the boy's chest. This episode, according to Hingley, shows that "the future dictator was aggressive from an early age."[8]

As a young teenager, Joseph's aggressive nature gradually matured and shifted from fistfights with peers to verbal attacks against adults. School records indicate that he was punished on several occasions for organizing protests against faculty and administrators whom he labeled morally weak and academically incompetent.

Joseph graduated from the church school in July 1894 near the top of his class. At his mother's urging, he applied for and won a small scholarship that partially covered the cost to attend the Tiflis Theological Seminary. He entered the school to study for the priesthood

Marxism

In the mid–nineteenth century, German philosopher Karl Marx published two revolutionary books, *The Communist Manifesto* and *Das Kapital*. In these two books Marx set forth the basic ideas declaring that history is principally determined by conflicts between the poor working class (such as peasant farmers and factory workers) and the wealthier ruling class (i.e., those who own the farms and factories).

Marx theorized that in industrial nations, as more and more wealth became concentrated in the hands of the ruling class and the poor sank deeper into poverty, the working class would grow ever more angry and resentful. Eventually, the poor would rally together and revolt against the oppressive wealthy class. That basic core of ideas, which was at the heart of the Bolshevik Party, quickly came to be known as Marxism and later communism.

Marx further theorized that, following a revolution, all class distinctions would be abolished and everyone would share equally in all the work and all the wealth of the nation. Marx's *Communist Manifesto* closed with these lines, which became inspirational to Bolsheviks and other revolutionary groups: "Let the ruling classes tremble at a communist revolution. The proletarians [poor] have nothing to lose but their chains. They have a world to win. Workingmen of all countries, unite!"

German philosopher Karl Marx outlined the fundamental principles of the political philosophy that became known as communism.

in the Georgian Orthodox Church. Keke worked hard to help him afford the tuition, still hoping that her son would mature and become a priest. Indeed, even years later, when Stalin ruled all of Russia, she told an interviewer that she would have preferred for him to have entered the priesthood.

○ As a young man, Stalin enrolled at the Tiflis Theological Seminary with the intention of becoming a priest in the Georgian Orthodox Church.

The Seminarian and the Marxist

The Tiflis Theological Seminary, although a religious institution, did not limit its instruction to church teachings. It was also Georgia's principal center of higher education, attracting students with diverse interest in all scholarly fields. Political and social movements were hotly debated there, and the seminary became a center of conflict between the strict conservative Russian Orthodox priests who administered the school and the more radical student body.

The conflict centered on the desperate plight of poor farmers. Peasant farmers complained about the economic gulf between themselves and the landowners, who kept most of the crop money. The peasants regarded anyone who did not work as a parasite, and they threatened a violent peasants' revolt unless the landowners handed the land over to them. The czar of Russia, Nicholas II, a member of the ruling Romanov family, autocratically ruled the nation. He rejected the peasants' demands and threatened violence of his own if their protests persisted. Many students, Stalin included, supported the peasants, while the priests supported the czar.

Stalin embraced a radical ideology aimed at the violent overthrow of the Romanovs. This ideology was called Marxism, named after the German philosopher Karl Marx, who encouraged poor workers to organize and violently overthrow the ruling class (in the case of Russia, the Romanov aristocracy) and take control of the nation. Following such a revolution, Marx contended, a more equitable distribution of wealth would occur that would dissolve the gulf between the rich and the poor so that all citizens could live more freely and share their nation's wealth more equitably.

It is not certain at what point Stalin abandoned his aspiration for the priesthood in favor of a Marxist revolution, but school records reveal a series of disciplinary actions against him for reading banned Marxist writings between 1896 and 1898. Despite the efforts of the seminary's administrators, Stalin and his classmates voraciously read antiestablishment literature that analyzed world history through the lens of Marxist thinkers. By 1897 Stalin began to refer to himself as a Marxist and by 1898 he committed himself to Marxist radical politics as a professional revolutionary working under the direction of Noe Zhordania, leader of Georgia's Marxist underground.

Stalin organized rallies and strikes and printed revolutionary leaflets calling for the violent overthrow of the Romanov family. One of the very few times that Stalin referred to his decision to become a revolutionary was many years later when he wrote to a friend, "I joined the revolutionary movement in protest against the outrageous methods prevalent at the seminary."[9] His disdain for the seminary priests was made evident one morning when he failed to rise from his seat as a sign of respect for a black-robed priest. The priest turned to him and queried, "Don't you see who is standing before you?" Stalin slowly rose, rubbed his eyes, and sarcastically replied, "I see nothing except a black spot."[10]

Stalin had clearly lost interest in the seminary and the politics of the priests who supported the czar. In May 1899 he was expelled, but the reason why remains unclear. He had taken part in radical demonstrations, expressed disrespect for faculty and administration, and refused to take required examinations. But according to one historical source, "Stalin was later to claim that the real reason for his expulsion was that he had been trying to convert his fellow students to Marxism."[11]

Rebel of the Caucasus

Now, at the age of twenty, Stalin committed his thoughts and energy to a revolution. In the winter after he left the seminary, Stalin took a job as an accountant at the Tiflis meteorological laboratory. This position would be the only conventional employment he would ever have. While employed for one year, Stalin used his weekends to roam Caucasus towns agitating among workers to embrace Marxist doctrine, helping organize strikes, and spreading Marxist literature.

He delivered his first pro-Marxist speech before a crowd of nearly two hundred workers in 1900. Although he failed to display great speaking skills or magnetism, he did show a talent for practical organizational activity. Stalin marked this significant turning point in his political life by dropping his childhood name Soso and taking the fiery name Koba, which was more befitting his revolutionary temperament. Koba was a much beloved Georgian outlaw as well as the name of a fictitious character in the Russian romance novel *Nunu*. The celebrated brigand Koba was known as a fighter for the rights of the working class; the fictional Koba was a man who willingly sacrificed everything on behalf of his villagers in his struggle against the czarist authorities.

Arrests and Imprisonment

In March 1901 the police raided the laboratory to arrest Stalin. He escaped out a back window but lost his job. He then became a professional revolutionary, as he would remain until the Russian Revolution in October 1917. After his escape from the lab, Stalin continued to work in hiding among the Tiflis Marxists

for another year, writing articles and organizing rallies, but his belligerent personality alienated most of his superiors and he was expelled from the group.

Undeterred, Stalin moved to the Georgian port city of Batum. There, in March 1902, he organized a Marxist march that drew the ire of local czarist officials. They sent the police to disperse the demonstrators. Moments after the police arrived, they fired into the marchers, killing fifteen and wounding dozens more. According to one eyewitness to the fracas, Emilian Yaroslavsky:

Comrade Soso [Stalin] stood in the midst of the turbulent sea of workers, personally directing the movement. A worker named Kalanadze who was wounded in the arm during the firing was led out of the crowd and afterward taken home by Comrade Stalin himself.[12]

Stalin was later identified as the leader of the marchers, seized, and shipped off to a Siberian prison four thousand miles from Georgia. After only one year there, Stalin escaped and returned to Gori; living in hiding was preferable to prison.

For the next few years, Stalin returned to his underground existence, and even though he was periodically arrested, he spent little time in jail. The Marxist Party in Georgia moved him from one "safe house" to another to keep him out of view of the czarist police who knew his face and were under orders to

In 1902 Stalin (identified in this photo with an "X") is arrested along with other demonstrators for participating in a Marxist march in the Georgian city of Batum.

arrest him. Living in basements and attics, Stalin was fed and provided with a desk and paper for writing leaflets and organizational plans for demonstrations. When he completed his work, others took it to underground printers and passed his organizational notes to activists responsible for their implementation.

Despite Stalin's disruptive and dangerous lifestyle, it was at this time that he married Yekaterina Svanidze, whose nickname was Kato. Kato was a simple peasant girl who loved Stalin very much and was devoted to his revolutionary ideals. She worked hard to make a home for them despite living in hiding and

Bolshevism

Founded at the beginning of the twentieth century, the Bolshevik Party, which was led first by Lenin and later Stalin, took its name from the Russian word for "majority party." After a number of years of rivalry with the Mensheviks, the minority revolutionary party, the Bolsheviks prevailed.

The Bolsheviks were a group of Marxists who supported Lenin's call for a party of professional revolutionaries. They believed in organizing the party in a strongly central-ized hierarchy that sought to overthrow the czar and achieve power. Although the Bolsheviks were not completely autocratic, they were characterized by a rigid adherence to the leadership of a central committee of powerful men selected from loyal Bolshevik members. The common workers were not allowed to vote.

It was the Bolsheviks' intent to orchestrate a takeover and extermination of the czarist government during a revolution and then become the rulers of Russia. During late 1917, when Russia was mired in the First World War, the Bolshevik tactical program excited the working class to revolt based on its slogan "Peace, Land, Bread." The lack of these three demands, which the czarist government was unable to meet because of the war, left urban populations starving on government-enforced rations. In October the Bolshevik-led revolution triumphed.

After the revolution the Bolsheviks banned Mensheviks and all other political organi-zations. They gained a reputation for dealing harshly with those they regarded as "enemies of the state," and it was their leaders who established the first prison camps known as gulags.

the arrests that came from conducting demonstrations.

In December 1905, while still in hid-ing, an important milestone in Stalin's career occurred. While actively involved in radical Marxist demonstrations in Georgia, he caught wind of a meeting that was being held by a relatively new political party in Russia called the Bolsheviks. The Bolsheviks were a group of revolutionaries intent on the violent overthrow of the czarist regime. Their belief in a violent revolution was based on Marxist revolutionary teachings. The Bolsheviks had been banned by the czar, forcing their leader, Vladimir Lenin, to meet with supporters in Finland to dis-cuss strategies to overthrow the Russian government.

Lenin had heard about Stalin's incar-ceration in the Siberian prison and his radical activities in Georgia. Lenin admired his willingness to confront the police, and he contacted the young revolutionary. After the exchange of a few letters, Lenin invited Stalin to the Finland convocation.

Stalin became an ardent admirer of Lenin, whom he viewed as a father figure. Stalin had earlier idealized Lenin as a "mountain eagle who knew no fear in the struggle and who led the Party boldly forward along unexplored paths."[13] Stalin was eager to attend the meeting.

He hoped to escape his underground life and make a more significant contribution than merely writing pamphlets in dark hiding places and leading violent street demonstrations. Stalin risked arrest by traveling by train to St. Petersburg and then across the nearby border to Finland. To avoid being detected, he donned a wig and traveled under the assumed name Joseph Ivanovich.

Chapter Two

STEPPING-STONES TO POWER

The meeting with Lenin in Finland was Stalin's first of many strategic stepping-stones to assuming absolute authority over the Soviet Union. Stalin arrived filled with high expectations for making his mark on the party. The meeting would introduce Stalin to the major figures in the party he would work with at a variety of tasks as he rose from a minor participant to a major party force and finally to the supreme leader of the Soviet Union.

Stalin's skills in leading violent demonstrations worked well in the streets, but they needed refinement for him to advance up the ranks of the Bolshevik Party. He still needed to acquire the more subtle skills of learning how to withdraw and remain in the background when situations warranted it, how

to disagree yet avoid direct confrontations with his superiors, and how to wait in ambush to destroy a rival.

The most critical element that Stalin needed for success was Lenin's support. Without it, Stalin understood that he would forever be one of hundreds of minor faceless party members working for more important men. He had no intentions of being a minor participant when the revolution came. Stalin's rise to power was so closely connected to Lenin's support that historian Christopher Read concluded, "Stalin's story would never have become important were it not for the fact that he had one, crucial, admirer—Lenin. At all stages, it was Lenin's hand that guided Stalin to high office. It was Lenin who picked him as a rising star."[14]

Stalin and Lenin in Finland

The initial meeting between Stalin and Lenin created an immediate bond of friendship. Lenin was attracted to Stalin's youthful rebellious behavior. Lenin was looking for revolutionaries willing to carry out tasks without fear of persecution or arrest. Stalin, meanwhile, was excited to meet the Bolshevik leader he had heard so much about.

Stalin was very impressed with Lenin's talent as a persuasive speaker. As an orator himself, Stalin understood the power of a well-structured, forceful speech. He came away from the meeting in Finland captivated by Lenin's style, as he later revealed in a newspaper commentary: "I was captivated by that irresistible force of logic in them [Lenin's speeches] which, although somewhat terse, thoroughly overpowered his audience, gradually electrified it, and then, as the saying goes, captivated it completely."[15]

Stalin (right) meets with Bolshevik leader Lenin in 1922. Lenin's support helped Stalin rise through the ranks of the Bolshevik Party.

Lenin's Early Life

Lenin was born Vladimir Ilich Ulyanov in 1870. He was the third of six children born into a close-knit family of educated parents. His mother, a housewife, was the daughter of a physician, while his father, although the son of a peasant, was a schoolteacher who later rose to the respected position of inspector of schools.

As a boy, Lenin was recognized by his teachers as intellectually gifted. His parents also saw this quality and encouraged his appetite for learning. He graduated from high school ranked first in his class and excelled in Latin and classical Greek. When he was sixteen, there was nothing in his personality that indicated he would one day be a revolutionary.

In 1887 Lenin entered college, and graduated with a law degree. It was at this time that he adopted the pseudonym Lenin while working as a revolutionary. In the early 1890s Lenin read the books of the Communist philosopher Karl Marx. Marx's ideas had a profound impact on Lenin, and he began to consider himself a Marxist committed to the violent overthrow of the Russian aristocratic family of Romanovs. By the mid-1890s Lenin preferred to associate with radicals who were inspired by Marx's ideas and he quit his law practice.

In August 1893 Lenin moved to St. Petersburg and began to associate with revolutionary Marxist thinkers. By the mid-1890s his brilliance and dedication to revolution was recognized. He quickly emerged as a radical intellectual and leader among followers of a Marxist revolution.

During the 1890s, Lenin (seated, center) became an avid Marxist determined to overthrow the czar.

This was also the meeting where Stalin met Leon Trotsky, Lenin's most trusted and influential Marxist friend. Stalin disliked Trotsky from the start because of his harsh and overbearing manner, traits that would eventually make Trotsky his archrival.

Honing His Revolutionary Skills

Following the Finland meeting, the twenty-six-year-old Stalin traveled back to Georgia with renewed enthusiasm for honing his revolutionary skills. In early 1906, inspired by his meeting with Lenin, Stalin returned to organizing anticzarist protests and writing speeches advocating a revolution. The more disruptions against the czar that he witnessed, the more certain he became of an approaching revolution, as he indicates in one of his emotionally charged leaflets:

> The Russian revolution is inevitable, and it is just as inevitable as the sunrise! Can you stop the sun from rising? Russia is a loaded gun at full cock, liable to go off at the slightest concussion. Yes, comrades, the time is not far off when the revolution will hoist sail and drive the vile throne of the despicable Tsar off the face of the earth! Let us join hands and *rally round the Party.*[16]

Stalin soon began to organize local railroad and oil-well worker strikes. His tactic was aimed at shutting down operations, which would cause owners to lose money. When the strikers were successful, owners were forced to increase workers' salaries to get them back to work. Strike violence often escalated when czarist police fired into crowds of strikers in an effort to disperse them. Following a violent strike at the railroad yards in Tiflis, Stalin proudly commented, "It was there that I received my second baptism in the revolutionary struggle."[17] (The first had been in Batum.) For his work, Lenin honored Stalin with his first party promotion to the highest position in the Georgian Bolshevik Party.

In November 1906 Stalin's wife, Kato, gave birth to a son, whom the couple named Yakov. Suddenly, and unlike most Bolshevik revolutionaries, Stalin experienced fatherhood. But within six months, tragedy struck when in April 1907 Kato died of typhus. Knowing that he could not care for his son and continue his radical activities, Stalin sent Yakov to be raised by his aunt and uncle. Her death was kept quiet—no official statement was made about Kato's death, although a rumor circulated that she had taken an overdose of sleeping pills. Stalin's friends later heard him express a rare moment of personal grief when he said, "This creature used to soften my stony heart. When she died all my warm feelings for people died with her."[18]

After his personal tragedy, Stalin added banditry to his list of underground

To help finance his revolutionary activities, Stalin participated in a series of bank robberies in Tiflis (pictured) and other Georgian towns.

activities. Professional revolutionaries had no legitimate sources of income, forcing many to turn to crime for financial support. Stalin took part in a series of daring bank robberies. In one raid in Tiflis he and his comrades seized a bag full of money but were caught and jailed for two years. He escaped within a year, but was rearrested and returned to jail.

Once he was released from jail at the beginning of 1912, Stalin was again rewarded by Lenin for his willingness to make sacrifices for the party. Lenin selected him to be a member of the Bureau of the Central Committee as director of revolutionary activities for all of Russia.

Lenin pointed to his tireless work and unswerving commitment to a revolution. In the opinion of historian Bertram Wolfe, "It was boldness in connection with deeds of individual terror that first attracted his [Lenin's] attention to Joseph Stalin and caused him to advance the latter [Stalin] to posts of importance."[19]

Stalin's Initial Disappointment with Lenin

Stalin's first meeting with Lenin in 1905 was historic; both men later became arguably the two most influential Russians of the twentieth century. In spite of the significance of the meeting, few details have survived. Historians are fascinated, however, by a rare note written by Stalin expressing his disappointment with Lenin's small stature and undistinguished features. Some historians believe that the note reflects Stalin's own self-consciousness about his own height— just five feet four inches—and his disfigurement from diseases and accidents. Other historians, however, view the note as a reflection of Stalin's excitement about meeting a hero he had so idolized that the actual meeting failed to measure up to the fantasy. The following expression

of disappointment by Stalin is found in Philip Pomper's book Lenin, Trotsky, and Stalin: The Intelligentsia and Power:

I was hoping to see the mountain eagle of our Party, the great man, great not only politically, but, if you will, physically, because in my imagination I pictured Lenin as a giant, stately and imposing. What, then, was my disappointment to see a most ordinary-looking man, below average height, in no way, literally in no way, distinguishable from ordinary mortals.

Stalin's initial reaction after meeting Lenin was one of disappointment with the Bolshevik leader's small stature and ordinary looks.

At the age of thirty-two, Stalin's rise in the Bolshevik Party, coupled with a closer friendship with Lenin, filled him with a sense of importance and authority. For his new position with greater responsibilities, Stalin departed the remote region of Georgia for St. Petersburg, the capital of Russia. Now that he had been accepted into the upper echelon of the party, he felt he needed a more powerful name than his nickname Koba. He dropped it in favor of Stalin, a Russian word meaning "made of steel."

A Changed Man Emerges

Stalin's personality changed in his new role as director of revolutionary activities. His new position required him to write articles for the official Bolshevik newspaper, *Pravda*, a Russian word meaning "truth." In this capacity, Stalin shed his rough exterior as a reckless street revolutionary and adopted a variety of clever techniques for promoting a revolution while at the same time promoting himself above his colleagues.

Stalin had boundless energy for publishing revolutionary articles and promoting himself. He wrote several stories a week advocating Bolshevik ideas about workers' rights, overthrowing the czarist monarchy, redistributing land to the peasants, and establishing an eight-hour workday for factory workers. He also wrote about strikes around the country and ideas for organized acts of civil disobedience in industrial cities.

Stalin also used the paper to target a handful of Bolshevik leaders whom he believed stood in his path to greater success. In a flare of attacks against these rivals, Stalin used his position to condemn them in *Pravda* articles. So compelling were Stalin's criticisms that several men were demoted or dismissed from the party. And when these men demanded the right to defend themselves in the paper, Stalin refused.

Stalin knew that his success depended on earning Lenin's respect. While Lenin was in exile in Switzerland, he read *Pravda* and generally approved of Stalin's articles but not those of other writers. In January 1913, following months of displeasure with what he viewed as an ineffective editorial staff, Lenin promoted Stalin to editor-in-chief of the paper, commenting:

> We must plant our own editorial staff in *Pravda* and kick the present one out. Can you call such people editors? They are not men but miserable dishrags and they are ruining the cause.[20]

As editor-in-chief, Stalin was emboldened to take greater risks. His increased sense of independence and confidence attracted a widening network of party members loyal to him. Knowing he had support, Stalin dared to criticize Lenin on occasion, but did so in a way that would not alienate the party's leader. Lenin more than once raged at Stalin yet

И. В. Сталин за составлением наказа
петербургских рабочих своему депутату

In this illustration, Stalin writes by the light of a lantern. In 1913 the future leader was arrested for publishing revolutionary articles in *Pravda*, the official Bolshevik newspaper.

did not fire him because of his ardent commitment to the revolution. In this environment Stalin learned to be a clever and skillful politician. Historian Philip Pomper provides insights into Stalin's behavior at that time, noting, "Stalin was one of those men of deep conviction who do whatever is necessary to achieve their end. He learned to avoid pitched battles with his superiors even when he opposed them."[21]

Unlike Lenin, czarist police were not tolerant of Stalin's writings. They made periodic raids on the *Pravda* offices and sent Stalin and others to jail or temporarily exiled them to remote work camps for publishing the newspaper. But in February 1913 this cat-and-mouse game ended when police dragged Stalin off in handcuffs for the articles he himself was writing.

Arrest and Exile

Stalin's punishment for publishing articles in *Pravda* was devastating to his career. He was sentenced to serve four years in exile in a harsh wilderness prison camp located near the Arctic Circle. The camp, which did not have bars or walls, was intended to do little more than isolate political radicals from their activities in big cities.

Although enjoying the relative freedom to roam around this frozen wasteland, Stalin saw no opportunity for escape. Years later, after returning to St. Petersburg, Stalin described this remote region as a place with "endless snow horizons, and frozen rivers where the sturdy, good-humored natives sit for hours on end at an ice-hole fishing."[22] Stalin also expressed the joys of indulging his boyhood love of nature. He took pleasure in hunting and fishing and talked excitedly about nearly being killed by a bear, and about how he almost froze in a sudden ice storm. He also confided that he lived with a local woman who bore a child by him.

In this grim Arctic outpost, participation in Russian politics was nearly impossible. He and Lenin exchanged a few letters discussing Bolshevik strategies and their hope for Stalin's quick return to St. Petersburg, but little else. During his exile, however, Stalin met other exiled revolutionaries. He met Lev Kamenev, a longtime trusted friend of Lenin. In 1914, when World War I erupted, both men expressed opposition to Russia's involvement in the war, agreeing that they would prefer to see the other European nations battle among themselves. Stalin met several members of the Menshevik Party as well. The Mensheviks were another group of Marxist revolutionaries who believed that a nonviolent revolution was possible by reaching a compromise with the czar, a notion rejected by the Bolsheviks, who clung to their idea of a violent overthrow and confiscation of land and factories.

In early March 1917 Stalin received word of the long anticipated revolution. In February a rebellion in St. Petersburg had forced Czar Nicholas to abdicate his throne. War casualties had been heavy since 1914, and shortages of food, medicines, and winter clothing needed by the troops left thousands to die in city streets. Protests in the streets and a mutiny by the troops forced the czar to abdicate in what has become known as the February Revolution. After the abdication, a provisional government was established as a temporary authority.

One part of the abdication agreement was a general amnesty extended to all political prisoners, both Bolsheviks and Mensheviks. Stalin and Kamenev rode a horsedrawn sled to the nearest train station to make the long return trip to St. Petersburg. When Stalin arrived, he telegrammed Lenin in Switzerland that he was back.

Lurking in the Shadows

Stalin awaited Lenin's return, along with all the other exiles, with the understanding that he would resume control over the Bolsheviks. Stalin consciously devised a new plan to remain in the shadows of more powerful Bolsheviks as

The Russian Revolution

The Russian Revolution of 1917 occurred in two stages. The first took place in February when starving people took to the street to protest against the czarist regime. The protests gradually grew and turned violent as large numbers of city residents rioted and clashed with police and soldiers. When the bulk of the soldiers quartered in the Russian capital joined the protests, they turned the protest into a revolution that forced Czar Nicholas II and his family from their palace and then forced his abdication.

Discontent smoldered and spread during the summer to more major cities throughout Russia. Suffering citizens were urged to action by radical Bolshevik agitators. And in late October and early November the second stage ignited when Lenin led his revolutionaries in a nearly bloodless revolt against the provisional government that had replaced the czar.

Peace, however, was short-lived. A civil war broke out in 1918 that pitted the Bolsheviks, known as "Red Russians," against conservative Russians who opposed the revolution, known as "White Russians." Following a bloody series of battles that cost millions their lives, the Red Russians prevailed and Lenin firmly established the dominance of the Bolsheviks.

Crowds flee as a gun battle between Bolsheviks and czarist soldiers breaks out on the streets of Moscow during the 1917 Russian Revolution.

Revolutionaries storm Czar Nicholas's palace in February 1917. They evicted the Romanov family from the palace and forced the czar to abdicate the throne.

a strategy for quietly asserting and gaining greater authority.

Stalin and other Bolsheviks had anticipated a revolution for years, but the February Revolution was not the one they had hoped for. Stalin was disappointed to learn that the provisional government was led by Mensheviks who had pledged to allow the Romanov family members to live out their lives in peace and had promised to continue the war

effort, two provisions unacceptable to the Bolsheviks.

Despite those disappointments, Stalin returned to resume his work with *Pravda* with a slight detachment that allowed him to direct activities yet remain in the shadows. This was a cleverly conceived strategy that became his hallmark as he rose to power. After four years in exile, many Bolsheviks found Stalin's manner abrasive and arrogant, and they resented his return as editor. Rather than confront them, Stalin cleverly stepped aside, allowing Kamenev to assume the paper's leadership. Stalin then quietly pretended to take a secondary role, although he was the one who actually wrote the editorials and controlled all published articles. Pomper correctly observes that "Stalin was playing a prudent waiting game in view of the unstable revolutionary situation."[23]

Trotsky also returned, to Stalin's dismay. Stalin and Trotsky had never formed a friendship, and the two often verbally sparred. Their disagreements usually focused on Bolshevik policies, but Trotsky's domineering manner also irritated Stalin. At this point in Stalin's career, he was beginning to evaluate potential rivals for their strengths and weaknesses. He knew Trotsky was Lenin's most trusted friend and it was that friendship, more than any other reason, that made Stalin jealous and resentful of Trotsky.

When Lenin returned on April 3, Stalin supported him in a second revolution, a Bolshevik revolution that would unseat the Mensheviks. Lenin respected Stalin and on April 29, at Lenin's urging, the nine-member Central Committee elected Stalin to its membership. This marked the first time that he had been elected to a high party post rather than appointed. Aware of how quickly Stalin had risen from a lowly street revolutionary to high officeholder, Lenin joked with him, "You know, to pass so quickly

from an underground existence to power makes me dizzy."[24]

Stalin could see that Russia was in ruins and ripe for a second revolution. By midsummer the war dragged on, causing more dissatisfaction than before the February Revolution. Loss of life, food shortages, and no relief in sight once again spawned clashes in the street between citizens and police. In August the situation worsened when soldiers mutinied in large numbers, throwing their support with the Bolsheviks because they were the only party opposed to continuing the war.

Disturbed by what he saw, Stalin used *Pravda* to denounce the Mensheviks as sympathetic to the czar and urged the peasants to join with Lenin and prepare for a second revolution. In late October, tens of thousands of demonstrators in St. Petersburg joined with the Bolsheviks to seize railroad stations, telephone companies, shipyards, and banks. Once the rebellion began, soldiers stormed the Winter Palace, where the provisional government was meeting, and drove its members into the streets. Lenin was hailed as the new leader of Russia, and the Bolsheviks firmly held power.

Once word of the Bolshevik revolution spread, other cities erupted in support. Not all cities supported the Bolsheviks, however. Several battles between Mensheviks and Bolsheviks broke out, but the Bolsheviks ultimately prevailed. Stunned by the success of the first Communist revolution, Western democracies headed by the United States and England sent an expeditionary army to crush the Bolsheviks. Recognizing that the Bolsheviks held most cities, however, the invading army withdrew. This abortive invasion was never forgotten by Stalin.

In 1919, following the Russian Revolution, Stalin was a rising star in the Bolshevik Party. He understood that having a wife would be an asset if he wished to socialize with the other leaders. So he remarried, this time to the much younger seventeen-year-old Nadya Alliluyeva, the daughter of a fellow revolutionary. Although Stalin had one son, Yakov, he had not seen the boy since sending him to live with his aunt and uncle. In 1921 Nadya bore Stalin another son, Vasily, and in 1926 a daughter, Svetlana.

The successful October Revolution meant that Stalin would once again be forced to skillfully realign himself in Lenin's party. No one questioned Lenin's leadership, but below him, friction between several key figures, most notably Stalin and Trotsky, heated up. Stalin seethed with anger upon hearing that Trotsky maliciously said in a conversation with party members, "Stalin never did any serious work,"[25] and later mocked him with the insult, "Stalin is the most distinguished mediocrity in our party."[26]

Stalin Secretly Builds a Cadre

Following the October Revolution, Stalin quietly strengthened his position in the party by secretly forming a cadre of Bolshevik friends. His motive, more than any other, was to eliminate Trotsky from Lenin's inner circle. Both men saw themselves as Lenin's most trusted second-in-command, yet only one could hold that position. To strengthen each man's claim as Lenin's most trusted adviser, each built a cadre of supporters.

Stalin engaged in a series of devious stratagems to build his cadre. He secretly promised key Bolsheviks special privileges and well-paying government jobs for their support against Trotsky. Stalin unethically made private deals offering the same political office to many individuals in return for their support. He also promised rewards that he could not deliver. He promised comfortable apartments, vacation retreats, private schools for children, and automobiles to those willing to support his views against Trotsky. According to Pomper, "All of them [Bolshevik leaders] had to resort to stratagems of concealment, evasion, and subversion. Stalin was a past master of all of these stratagems."[27]

In May 1922 Stalin made his boldest and most subversive move when Lenin suffered an incapacitating stroke. Stalin knew that if Lenin died, a power struggle for his position would ensue, and Trotsky would be the most likely successor. Bent on outmaneuvering Trotsky, Stalin acted to improve his position. While Lenin was recuperating, Stalin secretly established a troika, an agreement among three men, to rule in the event of Lenin's death. He secretly discussed the idea with two of his friends, Lev Kamenev and Grigory Zinoviev. Although Stalin chose the two men, he did not necessarily trust them; they were simply necessary to counter Trotsky's power. Stalin's decision was dicey. Lenin was the supreme authority and establishing a troika without his approval or knowledge would be an affront to that authority. But he knew that if Lenin's recuperation failed, Trotsky would be isolated and powerless against his cadre.

Lenin recovered and eventually learned of Stalin's power move. He was furious at Stalin's insubordination and turned against him. In Lenin's view, Stalin had used deception and coercion to create the troika. Lenin denounced him, saying, "Stalin has acquired immense power in his hands, and I am not certain he will always know how to use this power with sufficient caution. . . . Therefore I propose to the comrades that they consider a means of removing Stalin from the post . . . and give it to someone

Stalin (left) made a secret agreement with Lev Kamenev (second from right) and Grigory Zinoviev (far right) that the three would rule the Soviet Union after Lenin's death.

more patient, more loyal, more polite, less capricious, and more considerate to comrades."[28] Despite this warning, those loyal to Lenin failed to act. On January 21, 1924, Lenin died of a second stroke.

Treachery and Deception

When Lenin died, Stalin had already positioned himself as his successor. Still, Stalin had to remove Trotsky without angering party leaders. To avoid being accused of ruthlessly eliminating his rival, Stalin conspired to convince Kamenev and Zinoviev to do it for him.

While Stalin remained in the background, he convinced Kamenev and Zinoviev that the three of them could prevail if they attacked Trotsky. The two men agreed. They accused Trotsky of undermining Lenin's policies. Such accusations created an acrimonious struggle among the three, while Stalin quietly watched; by manipulating Kamenev and Zinoviev, Stalin appeared to be outside of this critical struggle. In January 1925,

at the request of Stalin, who falsely claimed that he was dissatisfied with the bickering of the three leaders, the Central Committee removed Trotsky from the party and exiled him. Stalin had defeated his archrival without risk to his position or reputation.

Stalin next targeted Kamenev and Zinoviev for elimination. Unbeknownst to the two men, Stalin met with small groups of Bolshevik leaders to disparage and accuse them of secretly supporting some of Trotsky's ideas that caused disunity within the party. The two men were expelled from the party and exiled from Moscow.

Stalin now stood alone without opposition. He announced his dominance to the Soviet people by renaming a great Russian city after himself. Lenin had done this just before his death when he renamed St. Petersburg Leningrad. In 1925 Stalin changed the name of the major industrial city Tsaritsyn, situated on the Volga River, to Stalingrad.

Chapter Three

The Great Terror

Now firmly positioned as the leader of the Soviet Union, Stalin needed to find ways to remain there. Employing treachery and deception worked well to acquire power, but maintaining it would call for different strategies. Stalin knew that he had enemies. Other politicians, especially supporters of Trotsky, were conspiring to cause his downfall. And they were not alone in their opposition to Stalin. Senior members of the military questioned Stalin's credentials as a military leader, and common workers opposed his Marxist economic policies.

To maintain his authority against all threats, Stalin employed a policy of cruelty and terror toward any who opposed him. Roughly between 1930 and 1938 (some historians believe 1932 to 1938), Stalin directed his secret police force to arrest millions of Russians who openly conspired against him, criticized him, or refused to conform to his policies. Many were executed; others were sent to prisons and forced-labor camps called gulags and never heard from again.

Terror tactics were also used against millions more who had little to do with Stalin; they did not disobey or criticize him or his policies. Stalin developed a deep paranoia and an irrational fear of threats, which drove him to eliminate even those who did not threaten or challenge his authority. Innocent people were regularly tortured until they confessed to crimes that they did not commit.

The reign of terror was so encompassing, brutal, and on such a large scale that historians later applied the ignominious title the "Great Terror" to this period. The term continues to be used. No other phase of Stalin's life is more

Women on a collective farm use machines to winnow grain. Collective farming was part of Stalin's program to modernize Russia.

closely associated with his tyrannical and murderous rule than this one.

Forced Conformity

In 1928 Stalin issued a set of Communist policies designed to turn Russia into a modern nation. He predicted that Russia would soon outproduce its more affluent European neighbors to the west. To achieve that highly optimistic objective, Stalin launched a policy of forced industrialization and farm collectivization. Under forced industrialization, the government seized and ran all private facto-ries, railroads, oil wells, and other privately owned businesses. Under farm collectivization, peasants were forced to relinquish their small farms to the government and work on the new larger government-owned megafarms called kolkhozy.

The collectivization program devastated farmers. Besides the loss of family-owned farms, collectivization prevented peasant farmers from leaving in search of work elsewhere. The effect of this restructuring was to introduce a form of enslavement into the countryside.

Although the program was intended to increase agricultural production, Stalin had a warped secondary motivation. After the October Revolution, wealthy farmers known as kulaks had opposed the Bolshevik revolution. Stalin had not forgotten their opposition and vowed to take revenge against them by taking away their farms.

Collectivization met widespread resistance from the kulaks as well as from poor peasants who refused to relinquish their property. Intolerant of those who would not abide by his directive, Stalin sent armed agents to enforce his policies. According to one Soviet source, by 1930 peasants fought back "with the sawed-off shotgun, the axe, the dagger, and the knife."[29] Thousands of peasants died fighting, and Stalin ordered the public execution of thousands more hoping to deter further acts of defiance.

Rather than submit, peasants expressed their hatred toward Stalin through acts of civil disobedience. They burned their own wheat fields and slaughtered their cows and pigs. Infuriated by farmers' refusal to accept collectivism, Stalin deported an estimated 1 million kulaks and other peasant resisters to gulags in Siberia. These gulags, which had been established by Lenin, were large camps where inmates toiled in miserable conditions performing hard manual labor such as mining coal, digging canals, laying roads, and building railroads. Most worked until they died of disease or starvation.

Resistance to the collectivization policies staggered the entire Soviet economy. Starvation in large industrial cities dating back to World War I and even the czarist regime continued rather than abated, as Stalin had promised. For many years, grain and livestock production sank below previous levels.

Stalin found himself under siege from inside his party and outside as the economy worsened. Rather than solve the problem by applying proven economic policies and practices, he forced workers to toil harder, live with less food, and cease all criticism or face his secret agents. One of Stalin's agents in the Ukraine sadistically commented that the repression of farmers was a great success because it showed the peasants "who is the master here. It cost millions of lives, but the collective farm system is here to stay."[30]

In an attempt to improve Russia's economy, Stalin erred a second time. In 1932 he increased grain quotas, the tonnage of grain guaranteed to foreign countries in exchange for machinery and factory equipment. Stalin raised this quota by 44 percent. The burden of this increase fell primarily on the Ukraine, a 233,000-square-mile farming region known as the Soviet Union's "Bread Basket."

Cruelty Toward Farmers

Stalin's increased quota was a devastating blow to the 35 million Ukrainian farmers. Struggling to adjust to life on kolkhozy, and reeling from violent clashes with

Stalin's oppressive agents, farmers failed to meet the new quota.

Stalin's response when he heard the news of the grain shortage was one of unprecedented cruelty. Rather than accept the shortage and adjust his wheat export quota, Stalin ordered his agents to fan out across the Ukraine and confiscate as much wheat as would be needed to meet the quota. Agents entered and searched peasants' attics, basements, and barns looking for hidden sacks of grain. When they found them, the sacks were carried off and the farmers punished by beatings and whippings. Stories of agents even taking baked bread from ovens were reported, as were the confiscations of indispensable seed grain essential for the next spring's planting.

Grain confiscations triggered a devastating famine in 1932 and 1933 that claimed the lives of between 6 and 8 million Soviet citizens. An additional 1 million were murdered or deported to the gulags. Historian Ronald Hingley, joined by many other historians, places the blame squarely on Stalin's shoulders, calling it "a Stalin-imposed famine."[31] The imposed famine, combined with Stalin's ruthless deportation policy, broke the spirit of Ukrainian farmers and forced those remaining into collectivization and submissive conformity.

In the midst of Stalin's cruelty toward Ukrainian farmers, his wife, Nadya, committed suicide. Between the time of their marriage and her death, Nadya sought greater independence and an escape from the dreary life as the wife to a malicious dictator. Earlier in their marriage, arguments between Nadya and her often drunken husband exploded, prompting her to distance herself from him and pursue a degree in chemistry at Moscow University. Stalin interpreted her independence as a betrayal and in 1932, following yet another argument, Nadya killed herself. The children were told that she had died of pneumonia, and she was given a grand state funeral. Rumors about her death, however, swirled. One alleged that Stalin had killed her because she found out about one of his secret lovers; another claimed that she committed suicide because a drunken Stalin told her that she was his daughter, a claim that could have been true. Stalin at one time had dated her mother, who was Stalin's age.

Stalin turned his attention back to the famine but refused to accept responsibility for it and for the problems with forced collectivism. Instead, he blamed tens of thousands of lower-level Bolshevik Party members. He claimed they had failed to properly implement his policies, used excessive force against the farmers, and intentionally undermined his efforts to increase production.

To ward off responsibility for the collapsing agricultural program, Stalin initiated the second stage of the Great Terror, aimed at purging the Bolshevik Party of those who he erroneously believed had failed him. According to historian Christopher Read, "The purges

The Children of the Famine

Few acts of Stalin's cruelty were more extreme than that of the famine of 1932–1933 that he imposed on Ukrainian farmers. The famine was especially cruel because small children suffered more than any other group. Stalin's agents who raided barns carrying away butter and sacks of grain destined for foreign markets left hundreds of thousands of Ukrainian children to starve. The tragic story of these children is told by several eyewitnesses.

One eyewitness to the starvation, whose remembrances can be found in Adam Ulam's book *Stalin: The Man and His Era*, said, "Many experienced great difficulties with provisionment. There were masses of people swelling up from hunger, and dying. Fathers and mothers tried to save their children, to save a little bread, and they were told [by Stalin's agents]: you hate your country . . . you are parasites, fiends, and reptiles. They took the grain but they would not give the grain to the starving children."

Another eyewitness traveling by train through the Ukraine recalled, "I saw the ravages of the famine of 1932–1933 in the Ukraine: hordes of families in rags begging at the railway stations, the women lifting up to the compartment window their starving children, which, with drumstick limbs, big cadaverous heads and puffed bellies, looked like embryos out of alcohol [medical] bottles. Starvation had wiped every trace of youth from their faces, turning them into tortured gargoyles; only in their eyes still lingered the reminder of childhood."

This photo projects a tender image of Stalin. At the time it was taken, however, hundreds of thousands of Ukranian children were dying of starvation.

Stalin's second wife Nadya committed suicide in 1932. The couple quarreled frequently, and Nadya killed herself to escape her unhappiness.

of many ordinary members can be attributed to the search for a scapegoat to avoid the blame falling on Stalin."[32]

Purging Disloyal Party Members

Stalin refused to accept responsibility for the Ukrainian debacle. By 1933 he had deflected criticism for the famine and the bloody resistance to collectivism by placing it at the feet of low-level party members. In an article he published in *Pravda*, Stalin denounced them. Most were shocked and angered by his allegations. Old-time followers of Trotsky emerged from hiding to blame Stalin for the failures, and others openly plotted against him. The majority, however, including many of Stalin's friends, cautiously whispered about the need to change leadership.

All who opposed Stalin knew by now that he had become increasingly indifferent and ruthless toward any who opposed or criticized his policies. For these reasons, most remained silent, waiting for a time when he would hopefully retreat and resign. Unfortunately, they did not know the man well. Far from retreating, Stalin became increasingly vindictive.

In 1934 Stalin launched an internal attack against fellow Bolsheviks that later became known as the Great Purge. This purge was a cleansing of the Bolshevik Party of all members who had at any time supported the policies of Trotsky, Kamenev, and Zinoviev; expressed sympathies with the kulaks; or failed to enthusiastically embrace Stalin's leadership. Although some quietly opposed Stalin and some of his economic policies, few, if any, of them dared to speak openly for fear of reprisals. Stalin expelled an estimated 4 million low-level and midlevel members from the party. Of these, almost 800,000 were executed, and 2 million more died from harsh treatment working in one of a growing number of gulags.

Stalin's belief that he was the target of a plot by a multitude of cloaked enemies had become a distortion of reality. At this point, he was suffering from increasing paranoia that prevented him from differentiating between those who might actually be plotting against him and those who were not.

Confused about how to respond to imaginary threats, Stalin even turned against high-level Bolsheviks. In 1934 he ordered the arrest and execution of 1,108 of the 1,966 delegates that attended the Communist Party Congress that year. All but 70 were executed without trials.

Stalin's ability to round up and exile or execute so many citizens was due to a massive secret police force under his direct control. This secret force, more than 1 million strong, was called, in English, the People's Commissariat of Internal Affairs, but was known to everyone by the Cyrillic alphabet initials NKVD. Without it, Stalin would have been powerless.

Stalin's Personal Army: The Dreaded NKVD

The NKVD was the secret police force that enforced Stalin's authority. Stalin used its agents to carry out his widespread terror. The charter of this secret organization, headed by Genrikh Yagoda, was to investigate all cases of high treason, espionage, and flight from the Soviet Union. Yagoda joined the Bolshevik Party in 1907 and was a close and trust-ed friend of Stalin. Secondarily, according to historian Robert Tucker, the NKVD's sinister powers were expanded to include arrest and detention of "all persons deemed socially dangerous. . . . The statutes made these crimes punishable by death." What made these statutes even more repressive was the law stating that family members of those found guilty were subject to five- to ten-year sentences if they knew but failed to

Conditions in Gulags

In 1919 Lenin ordered the construction of the first gulags, and by the end of the 1930s Stalin had expanded their number to over four hundred. Surrounded by walls of barbed wire, the camps were secretive and the living conditions extremely harsh.

Prisoners were given inadequate food rations, which caused the starvation of hundreds of thousands. Stories told by guards reveal that inmates received half the ration given to gulag guard dogs. According to one 1940 camp inspection, the entire lunch for a laboring convict digging ditches consisted of water, four ounces of grain, and three ounces of black bread. In addition, insufficient clothing, which made it extremely difficult to survive the bitterly cold winters and the long working hours, was a constant cause of illness and death.

Inmate abuse by guards was also commonplace. It is believed that about one-half of all inmate deaths each year were caused by extreme torture. Prisoners were deliberately struck with batons and thick flat leather straps as a form of torture intended to deter escapes or refusal to work. Some were tied overnight to posts, where during the hot summer mosquitoes would swarm them for hours; during the winter, prisoners suffered severe frostbite or simply froze to death.

One part of the torture for exiled families was the agony of separation. Wives were housed in separate barracks yet often shared the same work camps as the men and worked side by side with them. There were special camps for children separated from their parents, and mothers with their babies were separated from their husbands.

report the crimes and five-year sentences if they had no knowledge. These powers were collectively labeled by Tucker as "an instrument of wholesale repression."[33]

The NKVD was the most feared Soviet institution during Stalin's reign. The standard activity of the NKVD officers was to arrest anyone suspected of crimes or plotting crimes against the Communist Party. (Lenin changed the name of the Bolshevik Party to the All-Russian Communist Party and then finally the Communist Party.) The preferred time to make arrests was between 11 P.M. and 3 A.M. Acting during this time generally prevented the targeted person from destroying incriminating papers, notifying friends or family members, or escaping. Witnesses report that a dark car would drive up to an apartment house and three or four agents would enter the building. Then, they would knock at an apartment door. If no one answered, as was often the case at night, the agents broke down the door and dragged the suspect out to the car.

Following the arrest, NKVD agents broke prisoners down with intimidating interrogations. The interrogators were often men who had been selected for their violent sadistic nature. Questioning about alleged crimes could last several days and nights without sleep. Refusal to confess to crimes they did not commit triggered threats of arresting and executing family members. If such threats did not work, beatings were administered until prisoners signed confessions or NKVD agents simply forged their signature. One way or another, confessions were signed and innocent prisoners were often badly injured.

Victor Kravchenko, who witnessed the activities of the NKVD, testified in 1947:

> Hundreds of suspects in Leningrad were rounded up and shot summarily, without trial. Hundreds of others, dragged from prison cells where they had been confined for years, were executed in a gesture of official vengeance

Among the many communist officials Stalin had executed was Lev Kamenev, one of the dictator's earliest allies.

against the Party's enemies. Then came a series of official reports vaguely linking Nikolayev [an alleged conspirator] with present and past followers of Trotsky, Zinoviev, Kamenev, and other dissident old Bolsheviks. Almost hourly the circle of those supposedly implicated, directly or "morally", was widened until it embraced anyone and everyone who had ever raised a doubt about any Stalinist policy.[34]

Within a year of its inception, the NKVD virtually replaced the Com-munist Party as the most powerful organization in the Soviet Union. As it moved into high gear as an agency of repression, Stalin found its tactics of repressing criticism of his policies highly effective. For this reason, the work of the NKVD increased as Stalin's acts of tyranny intensified.

The Worst of Times

For the Soviet people as a whole, the years between 1934 and 1938 were the worst of the Great Terror. These were years of brutal, unrestrained police terrorism aimed at common citizens, old

Workers in Leningrad listen as an official informs them of the execution of Zinoviev, Kamenev, and fourteen other Trotskyites.

enemies no longer a real threat to Stalin, and even military leaders. By this time, Stalin had lost any sense of rational behavior.

Millions, mostly those living in major industrial cities, suffered in an atmosphere of paralyzing fear of arrest, denunciation, deportation to a gulag, or execution; many suffered all of them. Most were victims for no apparent reason other than Stalin's paranoia. And no one was above suspicion. One Soviet writer recalled, "We all trembled because there was no way of getting out of it [the terror]. Even a Communist can be caught. To avoid trouble became an exception."[35]

Some people were victims of terror for deviating from Bolshevik Party policy, known as the party line. Stalin was the man who set the party line that all were obligated to follow. The party line represented Stalin's views on all manner of things, such as the foolishness of believing in religion, which nations were to be reviled and which respected, the inherent superiority of a dictatorship over democracy, those Bolsheviks worthy of respect and those to be scorned, and even his ideas on family values and morality. Historian Steven Kreis commented on what might happen to those who violated the party line: "Stalin issued the 'general party line.' Anyone who deviated from that line was condemned to either exile or execution—in most cases, execution."[36]

In 1936 Stalin began what became known as the show trials, rigged trials staged before tens of thousands of people with the intent of deterring anyone from thinking about deviating from the party line or plotting against Stalin. Stalin first brought his old allies Zinoviev and Kamenev to a staged public trial in Moscow. An international press corps was invited to lend a sense of legitimacy to the proceedings. When their trial ended, Zinoviev, Kamenev, and fourteen others were all executed for expressing sympathies for Trotsky. In January 1937 a second great show trial was held in which seventeen leading Bolsheviks declared that they had knowledge of a conspiracy between Trotsky and the German and Japanese intelligence services. A crowd of 200,000 voluntarily packed Red Square in frigid weather to hear the reading of the death sentences. All seventeen were executed.

Stalin did not even bother to hold trials for lesser known enemies. For those people, Stalin limited investigations and executions to a maximum of ten days. Furthermore, there was no allowance for lawyers, appeals, or pardons. Stalin had, in effect, stripped all citizens of basic civil rights. According to historian Helen Rappaport, these barbaric standards worsened within a year when "three-man boards passed sentences of death after a mere 10 minutes of ritual paper shuffling, after which the accused would be taken away and summarily shot."[37]

Stalin also turned his attention to suspected enemies in the Soviet military. In 1937 Stalin began mass purges of the army high command, and by 1939 one-third of all officers, three out of five marshals, and fourteen out of sixteen army commanders were accused of spying for the Germans. They were found guilty, shot, and dumped in a trench on a construction site, all within eighteen hours. This reckless purge left the armed forces incompetent and leaderless, and left the country vulnerable to invasion.

Restricted Travel

Another component of Stalin's repressive policies toward his citizens was restricting their rights to travel within their own country. For the first time in the history of the nation, all adult citizens were required to carry an internal passport to travel beyond their home cities. Prior to departure from home, travelers were required to explain their reasons for travel to the secret police and receive a stamp on their passport indicating they had been given permission to travel. Travel beyond the borders of the Soviet Union was even more difficult because Stalin feared that citizens would see the prosperity and freedom in foreign countries and refuse to return home. Passports might be checked in airports, railroad stations, and dockyards. Without a valid passport stamp no one was permitted to purchase a ticket. Hotels also had the right to request a review of travelers' passports. Failure to produce a passport with a valid stamp was grounds for imprisonment.

During the 1930s, no citizens received permission to travel outside the country unless they were members of official delegations visiting foreign countries for military or diplomatic reasons. And even then, all travelers were required to travel in groups to discourage individual acts of defection to foreign governments. One strategy used by Stalin to discourage defection was to allow foreign travel only for those with family members remaining behind. If traveling members failed to return, those at home would be punished. In effect, this policy meant that family members were held as hostages until their traveling members returned. Soviet documents written during this period revealed that children as young as twelve years old were imprisoned when older relatives refused to return from foreign visits. Because of this policy, few dared to defect.

Crushed Spirits

A collective fear of arrest and deportation gripped the minds of the Soviet people and crushed their spirits. Stalin's increasingly irrational response to any criticism of his failed economic policies repressed people's willingness to express their misery, dashed hopes for their families, and made it difficult to find any simple happiness in their lives. Never knowing who could be trusted, few dared to discuss openly anything about their lives. Soviet writer Isaac Babel wryly remarked, "A man speaks openly only with his wife, at night, and with the blankets over his head."[38] Basic family and friendship instincts of trust, honor, respect, and decency were torn away by

Letter from a Gulag

Most gulag inmates were not allowed to write letters, and those who could write home faced censorship from guards. Still, some letters managed to get through describing the unbearable living conditions within. One letter found on the Web site Moreorless describes the first impressions upon arrival at the Solovetz gulag.

Upon landing on the Solovetz soil we all felt that we were entering a new and strange phase of life. From conversations with inmates we learned of the shocking regime which the administration is applying to them. There is no limit to their hours of servitude. They receive a real starvation ration, being fed largely with stinking codfish. Beating is practiced at every step upon the slightest pretext. Every keeper, barrack-warden, every petty official supervising the penal labor has the "right to the stick", i.e., the right to beat. The high officials do not even need such a right. They can beat whenever they like and with anything they please.

We are invalids, broken and crippled emotionally and physically. It is difficult for a human being even to imagine such terror, tyranny, violence, and lawlessness. When we went there, we could not conceive of such a horror, and now we return, crippled ourselves, together with several thousands. The former tsarist penal servitude system in comparison to Solovetz had 99% more humanity, fairness, and legality. People die like flies, i.e., they die a slow and painful death.

Stalin's orders to root out all conspirators, real or imagined. Family members became mutually suspicious of each other. The secret police went to the public schools, even at the elementary level, and asked the children to report any suspicious behavior on the part of their parents. Awards were handed out at school to children willing to denounce their parents even though they were not old enough to understand the consequences of their betrayals. Wives fearing that suspicions on the part of the NKVD about their husbands might implicate the entire family filed for divorce to save themselves and their children. Relatives of those deported to one of the gulags or executed were treated like pariahs.

Arrests for acts of treachery and irreverence became ludicrous in their absurdity. The NKVD arrested citizens for trivial reasons such as removing a portrait of Stalin from a wall, crumpling up a newspaper with Stalin's portrait, criticizing a colleague at work, and failing to arrive at work on time. However ridiculous the reasons were, once arrested, fathers and mothers often confessed to acts they did not commit to save their spouses and children from the same fate. Confessions also saved many from torture and severe beatings.

The psychological depression of crushed spirits was visible on the streets. Soviet citizens learned to walk quickly, keep their heads down, avoid eye contact with strangers, and avoid unnecessary conversations that might be overheard by spies. As one worker in Kiev recalled:

> Our way of life, that had been firmly rooted in our friends and families, vanished. We were set upon by our friends and fellow workers like dogs. We talked to them about nothing more than the weather for fear of the nocturnal knock at the door by the secret police. Everyone gazes at us with watchful eyes, even the children.[39]

By the time the terror subsided in 1938, Stalin had managed to bring both the Bolshevik Party and the public to a state of complete submission. Using the feared undercover NKVD agents, Stalin stifled all opposition and criticism. Ruling absolutely, Stalin gradually turned his attention to the West, where his capitalist enemies Germany, France, England, and Italy were making preparations for war among themselves. A possibility that such a war might spill over into his nation was beginning to distract Stalin from his repressive rule.

Chapter Four

THE SECOND WORLD WAR

The horrific suffering the Soviet people endured during the Great Terror gradually receded in 1938, but only because another tragedy was awaiting them. To the west, Adolf Hitler, a German dictator as violent and ruthless as Stalin, was threatening war with several neighboring countries, suggesting that a war throughout most of Europe was likely.

Stalin's earlier blunders had made the Soviet Union vulnerable should a war arise. His economic policies, especially in agriculture, had failed to elevate the Soviet Union to the heights he had promised in 1928. The Soviet Union lagged behind the rest of Europe in food production, industry, and communications. Stalin's executions of top military leaders also crippled the military's ability to fight effectively. Furthermore,

Stalin's restrictions on travel, which had isolated Russia from Western nations, prevented most Soviet leaders from fully understanding the threat that Hitler and his Nazi Party posed.

War Clouds over Europe

Stalin had focused little attention on any policy other than improving the Soviet economy and inflicting terror on his citizens. But in March 1938 that came to a halt when Hitler sent his German troops storming across the Austrian border without any country coming to Austria's defense. Stalin and other European leaders suspected that Czechoslovakia might be next. They were correct.

At the end of May, Hitler called for the German occupation of a large region in Czechoslovakia called the Sudetenland. Several western European nations, most

Adolf Hitler (center) meets with European leaders in 1938 to sign the Munich Pact, a treaty that allowed the Nazi leader to annex the Sudetenland in Czechoslovakia.

notably England and France, feared that Hitler would soon seize more of Europe unless he was confronted. They rushed their diplomats to the German city of Munich in the hopes of cooling growing war tensions. Following several days of discussions, Germany, England, France, and Italy signed the Munich Pact, which allowed Hitler to take the Sudetenland with the stipulation that this would be his last act of aggression. One day later, German troops occupied the territory. Six months later, however, German troops violated the Munich Pact and grabbed the remainder of Czechoslovakia.

Uninvolved and distant from the intrigues of western Europe, Stalin watched this political chess game with delight. His nation was the only Communist nation, and he hoped that a war pitting Germany against England and France would destroy the capitalistic systems of all three, leaving his nation unscathed. Stalin also despised Hitler, in part because of his anti-Communist rhetoric and in part because of his recent aggressions. In Stalin's mind, Hitler was as loathsome as the czar had once been.

Sitting in Moscow, a thousand miles from the worsening conflict, Stalin's strategy was to encourage Hitler to even greater aggression yet, at the same time, prepare for war against him by appealing to the French and English for help. This strategy, requiring a double alliance, would be Stalin's first—but not last—foray into international politics outside the Soviet sphere of influence.

Forging a Double Alliance

Stalin took charge of the threat of war. He was not content to sit back and allow his diplomats and generals to dictate Soviet policy and strategy. Stalin signaled both sides of his interest in an alliance. In so doing, Stalin secretly pursued an insidious double alliance, one with England and France against Germany and the other with Germany against England and France. Such a complex yet potentially risky diplomatic posture appeared to guarantee a victory for the Soviets regardless of which side won. Stalin astutely understood that his nation could play a pivotal role if war erupted.

Stalin first entered into diplomatic discussions with England and France because he feared that Germany might invade his poorly defended country. Stalin told England's Prime Minister Neville Chamberlain that the best way to deter war with Germany was to form an anti-German alliance. Chamberlain, however, was not enthusiastic about

forming an alliance with the Soviet Union because he distrusted Stalin. He knew that Stalin had delivered many speeches critical of England's capitalist economy, an economy that Stalin hoped and predicted would collapse. Both the French and English also doubted the Soviet Union's ability to mobilize its shattered economy to wage war against Germany's highly mechanized forces.

Stalin distrusted England and France as well. After all, both countries had capitulated to Hitler's demands for the Sudetenland. Stalin had reason to believe that the main objective of English foreign policy was to encourage Germany to head east across the Ukraine into Russia, rather than west into France and England.

At the same time that Stalin pursued secret negotiations with England and France, he sent his ambassador, Alexei Merekalov, to Berlin to negotiate with Hitler's ambassador, Joachim von Ribbentrop. Stalin was aware that Hitler feared an alliance between England, France, and the Soviet Union because those three could militarily surround Germany, forcing Hitler to fight a difficult two-front war. He also had secret information indicating that Hitler was on the verge of attacking Poland and did not want Soviet troops to intervene. Stalin therefore offered Hitler a nonaggression pact promising not to attack Germany in return for the same assurance. In addition, Stalin wanted Hitler to give him a part of Poland that was rich in oil; control of the Baltic States, Estonia, Latvia, and Lithuania; and the wheat fields of Bessarabia, most of modern Moldova near the border of the Ukraine.

The German dictator grudgingly accepted Stalin's offer. Edging ever closer to his timetable to invade Poland, Hitler sent Ribbentrop to Moscow to sign the treaty that Hitler needed more desperately than Stalin did. In the end, both men got what they wanted. As Ribbentrop signed the terms on August 23, 1939, Hitler was reported to have said, "Now I have the world in my pocket."[40] Meanwhile, Stalin secretly expressed his delight at what he believed to be a winning strategy for his nation.

Most historians view Stalin's decision to side with Hitler as an astute strategy. Stalin did not trust Hitler and recognized that Germany might invade his nation. Yet by signing the nonaggression alliance, Stalin, in effect, had bought time to prepare his country for war. At this point, Stalin quietly dropped further negotiations with France and England.

Preparing for the German Invasion

Stalin faced a Herculean task preparing his nation for a German assault. He had militarily weakened his own country prior to the German threat through his purges. His elimination of most of the Soviet army officer corps left few veterans with any battlefield experience to stop a German advance. Equally unsettling was the shambles of Soviet industrial and agricultural production.

Early in 1940 Stalin changed his view of a possible invasion to a certain invasion. He took charge of retooling Soviet industry to produce weapons and planned his strategy for defending the Soviet border. Stalin increased arms production with a fevered pitch. Factories producing heavy farm equipment such as tractors and grain trucks were modified to produce troop transport trucks, tanks, machine guns, and heavy artillery. Cotton and wool mills weaving cloth for civilian clothing began weaving army uniforms, blankets, parachutes, and tents. Airplane production focused exclusively on fighter planes that might be needed to stop a German advance. Stalin further deployed several new divisions of troops along the western border.

Stalin drove himself and his staff relentlessly seven days a week for sixteen hours a day. Stalin's administrator in charge of war preparations, Y. Chadayev, reported to Stalin on one particular phase of work, "Work is going on round the clock, it will be ready in two months," to which Stalin responded, "Get it finished earlier."[41]

Soviet civilians were yet again expected to make sacrifices. Food distribution was focused on the western front along with medicine, gasoline, clothing, freight trains, and a multitude of other critical resources. Ideological preparations were also placed in high gear.

Newspapers and films glorified the Soviet army, plays were written with military themes, and composers wrote songs about a speedy victory.

By the spring of 1941 Stalin and his staff succeeded in moving a formidable force to the western front fully supplied with tanks, artillery, and aircraft. He also had well-placed spies working in the German high command who supplied him with information indicating that German troops were massing along his border. Stalin now knew that war was inevitable and believed that his nation would prevail. Russia had a long history of defeating invading armies bogged down in Russia's punishing winters. Stalin was confident that his troops would defeat the Germans, as he noted on May 5:

It is a fact that Germany has a very good army, from the point of view of its armament, as well as from the point

Stalin (standing, second from left) looks on as Soviet Foreign Minister Yacheslav Molotov signs a nonaggression pact with Germany in August 1939.

Soviet tanks roll toward the battlefront to repel the invading German army in June 1941. Hitler was convinced his invasion of the Soviet Union would result in swift victory.

of view of its organization but the Germans are wrong in considering their army as invincible. There are no invincible armies. Germany can not win the war under the banner of conquest and plunders, under the slogans of subjugation of peoples and countries.[42]

Generalissimo Stalin

On June 22, 1941, the long-awaited German invasion, named Operation Barbarossa by Hitler, smashed across the Soviet border. Hitler sent over 3 million well-trained, battle-tested German soldiers and 3,300 modern Mark IV tanks against a 3.2-million-man Soviet army, only half of which was trained, and 20,000 tanks, most of which were obsolete. Hitler's objective was twofold: to destroy communism and annex vast areas of Soviet wheat and oil fields to Germany. The circumstances favored a quick German victory.

Moscow, Leningrad, and Stalingrad. In October 1941, when German troops were only fifteen miles outside Moscow, Stalin ordered the evacuation of most of the city while he remained with General Zhukov to direct its defense. Stalin made a public show of invincibility by preparing for the siege in a bombproof air raid shelter positioned under the Kremlin. From there, he and Zhukov directed the city's defense. By December 1941 the Soviet army forced the Germans from Moscow.

Stalin now turned to assist beleaguered Leningrad and Stalingrad. The Germans continued their assault on Leningrad despite their loss at Moscow. Cut off from the rest of the Soviet Union, hundreds of thousands of civilians in Leningrad starved to death while the Germans pounded the city with artillery. Stalin ordered the construction of a roadway across frozen Lake Ladoga that successfully supplied badly needed food and assisted with an evacuation of civilians.

As the battle for Leningrad entered its second year, Stalin and Zhukov added General W.N. Gordov to their command to counter Hitler's attack on Stalingrad. Each man knew that the capture of the city and its oil-rich region would be catastrophic for their ability to fuel their tanks and aircraft. The fighting inside Stalingrad was more brutal than at any other city. As winter deepened, the situation for the Germans worsened. Under relentless pressure from

attack by Gordov's frontline troops, the Germans surrendered in January 1943.

It was at this time that word came to Stalin that his first son, Yakov, had been captured by the Germans and executed. Stalin had seen Yakov on only a few occasions and had shown little interest in renewing his relationship with him after the fourteen-year separation that began when Yakov's mother died. Once the two got together, however, Stalin immediately despised him, and when the news of his death reached Stalin, he was heard to comment that his son had been worthless from the start.

Stalin felt more affection for his second son, Vasily, who was a pilot in the Soviet air force. He was more to his father's liking than Yakov even though he was a bully, a womanizer, and a drunk. Vasily used his name to get whatever he wanted. He was promoted in the Soviet air force even though he was considered little more than an adequate flyer.

Turning his attention back to the war, Stalin was feeling confident that the worst of the fighting was over. Following the liberation of Moscow and Stalingrad, Stalin concentrated his remaining troops in Leningrad, and in January 1944 they were victorious. Stalin subsequently issued an order to his generals to prepare for an invasion of Germany that would crush the nation and end the war.

Empire Builder

With the defeat of Germany assured, Stalin set his sights on expanding his

Winston Churchill (left), Franklin D. Roosevelt (center), and Joseph Stalin attend the Yalta Conference in February 1945 to discuss the future of liberated Eastern European countries.

nation's territory. To accomplish this and other secondary objectives, Stalin met with President Franklin Roosevelt from the United States and Prime Minister Winston Churchill from England to discuss the future of those nations occupied by Germany. Although Roosevelt and Churchill thought their independence should be returned, Stalin viewed them as prizes that would create a mighty Soviet empire.

It was during the meetings first in Yalta and then at Potsdam that Stalin emerged as a skillful negotiator capable of outmaneuvering his allies to achieve the settlement that he wanted. In February 1945 the three leaders met in Yalta to discuss the future of the liberated Eastern European countries: the three Balkan States, Poland, Hungary, Czechoslovakia, Romania, and Bulgaria. Stalin entered Yalta intent on taking

The Battle for Stalingrad

In the early months of 1942, the Germans' main objective was to capture Stalingrad. Stalingrad was a key strategic city because it provided the Soviets access to their oil supplies. Stalin, however, was prepared to defend the city at all costs.

In July 1942 the German army surrounded the city. In response, Stalin moved two entire armies of 100,000 men there. On August 19 the assault began and bitter fighting raged in the city. The fighting moved street by street and house by house. Soldiers on both sides fought with small arms from rooftops, in alleyways, and in the sewers running under the city. The Soviet Red Army fought and died for every inch of the city.

In an attempt to clear away hiding places used by Soviet defenders, more than a thousand German airplanes dropped incendiary bombs on the city. Stalingrad was an old city with many wooden buildings, gas tanks, and fuel tanks for industries. As a result, fires erupted throughout the city, destroying hiding places as well as the homes of thousands of people. One air raid of 550 planes started fires that killed 40,000 civilians.

In November Soviet reinforcements arrived and trapped about 300,000 Germans. Realizing their defeat, the German army of 23 generals, 2,500 other officers, and 90,000 soldiers surrendered on February 2, 1943.

The battle for Stalingrad is considered by many historians the turning point of the war because it was Germany's first major defeat and it showed the world that the mighty German war machine could be defeated. Following the victory, Soviet troops began the slow process of pushing the remaining invaders out of the Soviet Union.

Nazi soldiers are marched to prison camps following the Soviet victory at Stalingrad in 1943.

them. His principal motivation was to control them and use them as a military buffer zone to separate his nation from future military threats from England and France. In addition, Stalin wanted their natural resources of valuable mineral and oil deposits and agricultural lands.

Churchill and Roosevelt viewed Stalin's empire-building ambitions as a threat. Stalin's control of those nations would mean that the Soviet Union would increase by 100 million people and accrue trillions of dollars of valuable natural resources. The addition of these countries would make the Soviet Union a formidable economic and military power.

Exhausted from fighting for years far from home, and still fighting the Japanese, neither Churchill nor Roosevelt had the resources to oppose Stalin. To deny Stalin the territory he wanted might trigger a war that neither leader welcomed. Besides, Stalin's armies that were push-

Clement Atlee (seated, left), Harry Truman (seated, center), and Joseph Stalin (seated, right) meet at Potsdam in August 1945 to finalize postwar negotiations.

ing toward Germany already occupied eight nations. So, Roosevelt and Churchill agreed to allow Stalin's troops to remain in the nations but insisted on vague wording in a treaty that would allow each country to have some form of elections at the end of the war. It was clear to everyone at the time that Stalin would control those countries, a reality that was particularly distressing to Churchill, as Adam Ulam, a contemporary Russian historian, indicates: "Churchill viewed the whole process with a sinking heart. Britain after all went to war in 1939 to keep Eastern Europe from being absolutely dominated by Germany. Now Soviet hegemony was to be even greater than that which Hitler would have achieved."[45]

Stalin also insisted on the return of tens of thousands of Ukrainians and other Soviet citizens who had aided the German invaders during the war. Many Ukrainians, still resentful about the collectivization of farms and the famine of the early 1930s, had aided invading Germans. Still thousands more from throughout the Soviet Union who had fled the country to avoid the war now wished to return. It was Stalin's intent to punish these people for what he viewed as traitorous acts.

Stalin got everything he wanted. British foreign secretary Anthony Eden noted Stalin's success as a negotiator: "Stalin is the only one of the three who has a clear view of what he wants and is a tough negotiator."[46] Eden later confided that if he were ever asked to pick a negotiating team to support him in the future, he would want a man like Stalin—shrewd and tough—to head it.

Between July 17 and August 2, following the collapse of Nazi Germany, the three world leaders (President Harry Truman replaced Roosevelt and Clement Attlee replaced Churchill) met again in the city of Potsdam, a suburb of Berlin, to wrap up final negotiations. When the meetings opened, Stalin made it clear that he had no intentions of limiting his empire building to Europe. High on his list of issues to negotiate was the ongoing war with Japan. Although it was clear that Japan was close to defeat at the hands of American forces, Truman was interested in any help he could get. Stalin expressed a willingness to divert Soviet troops from Germany to fight the Japanese in exchange for the Sakhalin and Kuril islands that lay off the coast of Japan. In 1947 the islands became a Soviet territory.

During the Potsdam negotiations, Stalin relaxed and expressed more of his personality than when he was in Moscow. He seemed to enjoy himself, displaying unusually good humor and polite straightforward conversation. Attlee commented on these qualities, noting that "Stalin could make jokes and take jokes" and that "he was a man you could do business with."[47] Truman also sensed that Stalin could be trusted: "You could talk to him straight from the shoulder."[48]

The Polish Killing Fields

In the spring of 1940 Stalin ordered his troops to occupy a portion of Poland. But Poland's proud history of independence galvanized the population to resist the Soviet invaders. Impatient to secure Polish oil fields, Stalin ordered the NKVD to round up anyone who might resist the occupation.

NKVD agents infiltrated the population looking for resistance fighters. They discovered widespread opposition to Soviet domination in the Polish army reservists. The reservists included thousands of the country's intelligentsia such as lawyers, doctors, scientists, educators, and businessmen who were called to active service by the Polish government. Once the NKVD identified those who vowed to resist, they arrested and isolated them from family and friends.

Under Stalin's orders, the NKVD marked fifteen thousand of these Poles for extermination. One-third of the group was trucked into the Katyn Forest, where each was gagged, bound, shot once in the head, and buried in a large communal grave. The remaining two-thirds were taken to other locations where they were executed in a similar manner.

These mass exterminations, which killed off much of Poland's intelligentsia, facilitated the Soviet takeover of Poland. Without the intelligentsia to publish anti-Soviet newspaper articles, organize resistance fighters, and educate the people about the Soviet threat to their independence, Poland became a vulnerable and leaderless nation.

When all the details were agreed on and the document signed, a gala party was held, during which Stalin dressed in an all-white uniform heavily decorated with gold braids and a dazzling display of medals. Observers commented that his dress and demeanor made him appear to be the preeminent leader of the three and the man most enjoying the celebration. It would be the last moments of warm relations between the three countries.

Stalin emerged more powerful than ever. His negotiating prowess made it possible for him to plant the flag of the Soviet Union high over Berlin as well as over all of Eastern Europe and islands he acquired off the Pacific coast. Stalin now controlled more territory, more people, and more natural resources than any of his predecessors and any of his adversaries at Yalta.

Stalin was hailed as a hero by his people. After seven difficult years of successfully directing the war and postwar negotiations, Stalin was idolized by a majority of Soviets. Photographs of Stalin standing with American and

British leaders with captions reading "The Big Three" were front-page news. Soviet spirits soared with the hopes that their country would emerge from past poverty and repression and stand as an equal with the mightiest nations.

Intrigued by his popularity, Stalin enjoyed seeing his cult of personality soar. He encouraged this hero worship by exaggerating his importance during the war. In a short time, he was promoting the fantasy that the war had been won because of him and no one else. Never a man to mix with the public, he now enjoyed occasionally waving to admiring crowds from his office window or from his seat high above parade routes.

While enjoying from a distance the adulation of the Soviet people, Stalin nevertheless recognized that America was emerging as an economic and military threat to his nation.

Chapter Five

The Terror Returns

The workers and soldiers who suffered most during the war surely thought that their reward for victory would be time to heal, relax, and enjoy a better life. The Russian poet Alexis Surkov summed up the feeling of millions when he wrote in 1944, "After the victory we shall call a halt, drink a cup, and rest to our heart's desire."[49] The hopes of the common man and woman, however, were not shared by Stalin. Within four months of the peace treaty, his domestic policy of terror returned.

Stalin faced a Soviet economy that had been devastated in the war even though his nation had been victorious. Stalin saw many of the same economic failures that had plagued his country prior to the war in addition to new ones. Many major cities—most notably Kiev, Leningrad, Moscow, and Stalingrad—

required major rebuilding. Factories lay in twisted ruin from German artillery attacks. Roughly a quarter of the country's resources had been destroyed, and industrial and agricultural output in 1945 fell far short of prewar levels. The loss of an estimated 20 million soldiers and citizens bled the country of badly needed workers for the rebuilding process that lay ahead.

The Soviet military was also in shambles. Contact with Allied soldiers of the American army in Germany showed Soviet generals that America's military was far better equipped with superior weaponry. But the greatest military concern to Stalin was America's development and use of the atomic bomb against Japan. Stalin wanted the same atomic capability to gain military parity with the Americans.

The financial costs of all of these undertakings, both civilian and military, would be staggering in terms of increased steel, coal, wheat, oil, and uranium production. The number of lives Stalin's over-ambitious policies destroyed was horrific. To most Soviets, it looked like the tough times of the 1930s might return.

Before addressing the problems of rebuilding the economy and the military, however, Stalin turned his attention to groups of Soviet citizens who he believed acted as traitors and enemies of the Soviet Union during the war.

Dealing with the Traitors

From Stalin's point of view, wartime traitors were a disease that had to be eliminated before infecting more Soviets. And to Stalin, consistent with his sense of paranoia, traitors were everywhere. Stalin was particularly incensed by Soviet prisoners of war (POWs) who had violated his order to die fighting rather than retreat or surrender. He also planned to punish Soviet partisans, primarily Ukrainians, who sided with the invading Germans. Also targeted were those who had fled to the safety of Western nations

Russian POWs liberated by Allied troops in 1945 appear jubilant in this photo. After returning to the Soviet Union, however, these soldiers were condemned by Stalin as traitors.

A Twisted Psyche

Stalin believed that the Communist Party and Soviet society were filled with people hostile to the revolution and to him. These were people he imagined, people who he believed hid their hostility behind appearances of loyalty and devotion to him. Everywhere Stalin went he seemed to encounter perceived enemies and spies. His urge to reveal these potential traitors and prove himself correct motivated his overpowering need for people to confess their disloyalty to him, thereby providing hard evidence that people he suspected of being enemies were in fact enemies, even if they were not.

Russian novelist Boris Pasternak recognized other aspects of Stalin's twisted psyche. His observations can be found in *1937: Stalin's Year of Terror* on the World Socialist Web site:

"I think that collectivization was a mistaken and unsuccessful measure, but it was impossible for Stalin to admit the mistake. In order to hide the failure, it was necessary

to use all means of terror to make people forget how to think and to force them to see what didn't exist, or to prove the opposite of what was obvious. Hence the unbridled cruelty of the Great Terror."

Pasternak was not alone in his assessment. On the same Web site, Russian writer Boris Nikolaevsky agreed with Pasternak that "Stalin had lost his mental stability, he lost the sense of moderation and he turned into a man who had lost his grasp of reality. The Great Terror was wholly a product of Stalin's paranoia, i.e., of a chronic mental illness expressed in the pursuit of maniacal obsessions."

Russian novelist Boris Pasternak wrote about Stalin's twisted psyche.

for the war's duration and were now returning.

Millions of newly liberated prisoners of war who had suffered for years in German POW camps yet lived to see their country victorious emerged malnourished and emotionally dejected. Stalin's hatred of these men was so extreme that their fate would be to exchange the horrors of Nazi POW camps for equally cruel conditions in one of Stalin's four hundred gulags. Most soldiers hoped that the American army invading Germany from the west would liberate them before their own Soviet comrades coming from the east because they knew they would receive better treatment from the Americans.

Stalin humiliated these men by forcing them to march all the way back home; according to Stalin, trains were for soldiers, not traitors. Russian writer and witness to the war Aleksandr Solzhenitsyn saw the seemingly endless line of weary emaciated men and described them as "the downcast columns of returning war prisoners, the only people around who were grieving and not celebrating."[50] Once back home, those fit to work were exiled to distant gulags, where they toiled until they died. Those unfit for work were shot. Over a million foot soldiers and 126,000 officers were sent to gulags. In this regard, Hingley noted, "Thus did many a newly 'liberated' Soviet prisoner of war immediately exchange Hitlerite for Stalinist captivity."[51]

Also despised by Stalin were those citizens who had fled the nation during the war and returned once it was over. To Stalin, such cowardice would not be rewarded. Most of those who departed lived along the western border and simply entered German-occupied countries to await war's end. Their thought was to return if the Soviet army prevailed but stay if it was vanquished. As these refugees trickled back, Stalin ordered his NKVD agents to intercept them, gather them up, and send them to the gulags.

Return of Stalin's Paranoia

It was also at this time that Stalin's paranoid behavior reemerged. Stalin was enraged when he learned that many of his soldiers and some citizens had struck up friendships with Americans. Stalin had always harbored resentment for Western capitalist nations because their more robust economies were able to offer more opportunities, consumer goods, and higher living standards than his Communist economy could. Stalin feared that returning citizens who had associated with Americans might be impressed with capitalism and criticize Stalin for his sagging Communist policies.

Many loyal returning officers and soldiers, those who had fought hard and not surrendered, were segregated from the rest because they were accused of associating with allied soldiers in Berlin. This segment of the victorious Soviet army, Stalin suspected, had heard corrupting stories of a more affluent life in America where grocery stores were filled with food, working-class families owned houses and cars, and the secret police did not exist. Stalin accused these soldiers of low moral standards, political weakness, and corruption because they had fraternized with the capitalist enemy. Stalin ordered his staff to determine which officers and soldiers appeared to have spent too much time socializing with Americans. A list was drawn up, and those on it were interned in gulags to keep them from "infecting" the population with subversive ideas about democracy and capitalism, twin evils to Stalin.

Soldiers were not the only Soviet citizens who were isolated for associating with Westerners. During the war, a number of American and British diplomats and military strategists stationed in the Soviet Union met and married Soviet women. Following the war, no amount of pleading could convince Stalin to issue the women the passports they needed to exit the country as their husbands departed. As historian Adam Ulam noted in his book *Stalin: The Man and His Era*, "Stalin would not let these 'unpatriotic' women flee to easy life abroad, babble slanderous tales about Soviet reality. Only after his death was this policy, more amazing in its pettiness than its inhumanity, reversed."[52]

Displacing Ethnic Populations

If Stalin's drastic actions against his own soldiers bothered many of his support-

ers, his treatment of select Soviet ethnic groups stunned them. Stalin's fury focused on ethnic groups living in north Caucasus, the Crimea, and the Ukraine. He was enraged at them because during the areas' occupation by the Germans, several countries had been offered independence if they would conspire against the Soviets. Although some did, many did not. Seeking revenge, Stalin sent the NKVD into several Soviet republics that had been penetrated by the German army and shipped entire populations from where their families had lived for many generations.

On February 25, 1945, leaders of the NKVD reported that 342,647 Chechens, people living north of Georgia, were loaded onto gulag-bound trains, and four days later an additional 135,832 were added. The NKVD raids were so secretive, well organized, and well executed that few families could escape, a fact noted in one official NKVD report: "There were only isolated cases of attempted flight."[53]

Stalin's wrath was particulary severe against the Ukrainians. Thousands of Ukrainians had formed an army called the Galicia Division that fought side by side with the Germans against the Soviet army. Besides, Stalin still harbored hatred for the Ukrainians for defying his orders to collectivize their farms during the early 1930s.

Stalin ordered the execution of thousands from the Galicia Division and ordered the forced deportation to gulags of more than a million Ukrainians who continued to embrace a hatred of Stalin from the early 1930s. As a way of emphasizing Stalin's irrational anger and the extremes to which he would go to exact revenge on his own people, Hingley notes that the Ukrainian deportations would have been far worse if Stalin had had more railroad cars on hand:

Lives Without Feelings

Stalin's ruthless purges and reign of terror fostered a troubling sense of anxiety among tens of millions of citizens who feared what might happen next or what family member might suddenly disappear in the dead of night. The Russian poet Osip Mandelstam expressed his country's fears while living under Stalin's oppression in the 1934 poem "We Live, Not Feeling," which makes several indirect references to Stalin and the fear he inflicted. This poem can be found on the Web site History Guide, reprinted in an article by Steven Kreis called "The Age of Totalitarianism: Stalin and Hitler."

We live, deaf to the land beneath us,
Ten steps away no one hears our speeches,

All we hear is the Kremlin mountaineer,
The murderer and peasant-slayer.

His fingers are fat as grubs
And the words, final as lead weights, fall from his lips,

His cockroach whiskers leer
And his boot tops gleam.

Around him a rabble of thin-necked leaders—
fawning half-men for him to play with.

The whinny, purr or whine
As he prates and points a finger,

One by one forging his laws, to be flung
Like horseshoes at the head, to the eye or the belly.

And every killing is a treat
For the broad-chested Georgian.

That the total number of persons arrested in the immediate post-war period was enormous we know; that it would have been even greater if Stalin could have had his way, we also know. But even the beloved Leader was compelled to adjust his appetite for repression to the technical possibilities of his age. Otherwise he would have deported the Ukrainians—all forty million of them—*en masse;* how fortunate, then, that insufficient rolling stock [trains] was available for the purpose.[54]

Stalin's deportation of entire populations to gulags accomplished more than simply eliminating those who threatened his authority. It also proved to be the source for repopulating the gulags with fresh inmates to work on new forced-labor projects.

Repopulating the Gulags

During the war, the populations of forced-labor camps declined precipitously. Inmates were released to work on one of dozens of war-oriented projects or were sent to the front lines to fight. Stalin's compulsion to eliminate entire ethnic populations quickly refilled the prisons. When the war ended, trains, trucks, and boats filled with "traitors" of one definition or another from throughout the Soviet Union poured into Stalin's gulags.

Stalin's ambitious rebuilding plan to repair Soviet cities, factories, and lines of transportation and communications required millions of laborers and vast sums of money. To save money yet still quickly rebuild his nation, Stalin ordered gulag crews of thousands of men to complete manual-labor projects such as building barge canals using only simple tools such as picks, shovels, and wheelbarrows rather than using expensive and scarce machinery needed by farmers and factory workers. The men worked until they died, and those who died were replaced at no cost to the government.

Stalin also forced gulag inmates to mine for a variety of crucial minerals such as coal, copper, gold, and uranium found in harsh climates. Other large engineering projects performed by inmates included constructing railroad lines, numerous hydroelectric stations, and roads and industrial complexes in remote regions. Intent on rejuvenating his nation's economy, Stalin continually increased the number of projects, which increased the need for more prisoners.

Stalin's quest to purge the Soviet Union of all who threatened his authority was not limited to large population groups sent to gulags. Following the war, his distorted thinking also focused on a few of his military leaders who had become public heroes for their roles in defending the nation against the Germans. A critical part of maintaining Stalin's cult of personality, which elevated him to the pinnacle of public adulation, was to prevent anyone else from approaching his fame.

Buildings from a Soviet gulag still stand in the town of Pevek. After World War II, Stalin quickly repopulated the country's gulags.

Jealousy and Suspicion

The victory over Germany elevated several Soviet generals to the status of public heroes. To Stalin, who suspected and distrusted anyone who achieved greatness, such hero worship was a threat to his position. As the war closed, two generals in particular threatened Stalin's cult of personality and his supremacy: General Zhukov and General Gordov. These two generals commanded most of the Soviet army. If both chose to turn against Stalin and ordered their troops to march on Moscow, Stalin would be unable to defend himself. Aware that any conspiracy against him would most likely come from the army, Stalin acted to eliminate both men.

The brilliant military strategist most deserving of accolades for engineering Hitler's defeat was Zhukov. He was the one who devised the plan to drive the

German invaders from Soviet soil and then lead the Soviet forces into Germany to capture Berlin. Stalin was so pleased with his performance at the time that he promoted him to commander of Soviet occupation forces. In Berlin, American and British generals praised Zhukov as one of the great strategists of the war.

Stalin's jealousy surfaced when he heard about Zhukov in Berlin and ordered him home. Since he was already well liked back home, Zhukov returned to Moscow to a hero's welcome in a ticker-tape parade. Stalin publicly acknowl-edged Zhukov's contribution to the Soviet victory but secretly was growing weary of his growing fame. Stalin asked the head of the NKVD to concoct a case of conspiracy against the great general. But as the trumped-up conspiracy case went forward, Stalin realized that Zhukov might be the one man too beloved to execute. Instead, Stalin demoted him and relegated him to a minor military post in the Ural Mountains.

General Gordov, the popular hero of Stalingrad, did not get off so easily. Stalin

General Georgi Zhukov (third from left) celebrates the end of World War II with Allied commanders. After the war, Stalin assigned Zhukov to a minor post in the Ural Mountains.

knew of his popularity in the city and, because of his jealousy, ordered the NKVD to hide a microphone to record conversations between Gordov, his wife, and General Rybalchenko. During these conversations, Gordov said things about Stalin such as "The way things are now you might as well lie down and die. Everybody is fed up with his life. Everything depends on bribery and bootlicking nowadays. . . . Why do I have to go to Stalin—why do I have to beg and demean myself?"[55] Stalin heard these comments and acted swiftly. All three were arrested and shot.

Stalin felt threatened by well-known nonmilitary leaders as well. The Soviet Union had many world-renowned intellectual and artistic celebrities whom he was willing to tolerate so long as they produced works consistent with his cult of personality. He recognized the propaganda value of writers, poets, painters, and musicians who positively portrayed him. Those who dared to attack Stalin, however, could expect some form of punishment.

Purge of Artists and Intellectuals

Part of Stalin's success was his use of propaganda to control people's thoughts. Stalin cleverly protected and crafted his public image as a solid and trustworthy leader by controlling newspaper stories, plays, books, movies, and paintings, all of which favorably depicted him. Those artists and intellectuals who refused to comply with his form of propaganda and

censorship, and there were many, found themselves on a train bound for a gulag.

In 1946 Andrey Zhdanov, a close associate of Stalin, helped launch an ideological campaign designed to demonstrate the superiority of communism over capitalism in all respects. This campaign, which became known as the Zhdanov era, attacked writers, composers, economists, historians, and scientists whose work allegedly manifested Western influence. The cultural purge continued for several years, stifling Soviet intellectual development. Stalin demanded that Soviet writers adhere to the principle of "party spirit," meaning they were expected to follow closely the views laid down for them by the Communist Party.

Stalin at times personally participated in the purge of artists. The opera *Lady Macbeth of Mtsensk* by the great composer Dimitri Shostakovich enjoyed great success until Stalin attended one of the performances and walked out. The following day an editorial critical of Shostakovich's opera appeared in *Pravda* with the title "Chaos instead of music."[56] The author was Stalin himself, and his review closed the opera and nearly cost Shostakovich his life. Musicologist H. Schonberg commented about Stalin's fear of Shostakovich's music: "Stalin banned it on the grounds that it represented decadent imperialistic capitalistic formalism. The country was closed to the rest of the world, composers and audiences alike did not know anything about contemporary music in the West."[57]

Russian composer Dimitri Shostakovich performs in 1956. The pianist was one of many artists and intellectuals whose careers were ruined by Stalin.

Perhaps the most well known writer to suffer at the hands of Stalin was Aleksandr Solzhenitsyn. He fought in the war, achieving the rank of captain of artillery, but was later arrested for writing a letter in which he criticized Stalin. His punishment was to spend eight years in a gulag and three more years in forced exile. In 1973, as a result of his experience, Solzhenitsyn published the most comprehensive book ever written about life in the gulags called *The Gulag Archipelago*.

The Last Terror

In October 1952 Stalin began preparations for a new terror aimed at Jews. This purge, known by historians as the Doctors' Plot, began when Stalin accused nine doctors, six of them Jews, of plotting to poison and kill the Soviet leadership. The innocent men were arrested and, at Stalin's personal instruction, tortured in order to obtain confessions. Stalin commanded the interrogators to "Beat, beat, and again beat," adding that if the torturer could not extract the need-

Stalin's Cult of Personality

The year after World War II ended, Stalin ordered a huge celebration and parade in Moscow's great Red Square to honor the nation's heroes. Stalin placed himself at the head of the list. As tens of thousands of troops marched by, all saluted Stalin as they passed. Millions of citizens lining the parade route cheered them while holding poster-sized photographs of Stalin with the title "Generalissimo" printed on the bottom.

Historians and sociologists studying this incident of self-adulation (and others that followed) explain it by citing the phenomenon known as the cult of personality, a term that derogatorily refers to the blind worship of a leader out of a sense of fear rather than love and respect. This cult of personality was carefully cultivated by Stalin and leaders of the Communist Party to focus the individual citizen's dedication and loyalty on the all-powerful leader who could be trusted to see the nation through times of great difficulty.

During the peak of Stalin's reign, he appeared as a godlike omniscient ruler, destined to rule the nation for all eternity. He adopted a number of informal self-congratulatory titles such as "shining sun," "the staff of life," "great teacher and friend," and "the hope of the future for the workers and peasants of the world."

Government orders prescribed the hanging of Stalin's portraits in every home and public building; artists and poets were instructed to produce only works that glorified him; and several cities such as Stalingrad were renamed after him. To justify this level of worship, Stalin presented himself as humble and modest, and would often characterize his vast personality cults as nothing more than spontaneous shows of affection.

Enormous portraits of Lenin and Stalin hanging from a Moscow building dominate this photo of a 1951 parade in Stalin's honor.

ed confessions, "We shall shorten you by a head."[58]

Confessions flowed from the doctors, providing the information Stalin needed as a pretext to attack all Jews living in the Soviet Union. As was the case twenty years earlier, family members and friends betrayed each other thinking they would save their own lives. Leading newspapers such as *Pravda* carried the story of the confessions, prompting the dismissal of thousands of Jews from their jobs, expulsion of children from schools, and the loss of housing.

Stalin intended to organize anti-Semitic attacks around the country, after which prominent members of the Jewish community would publicly beg him to protect the Jews by sending them to Siberian gulags rather than execute them. Plans to deport the Jewish population were discovered when 1 million copies of a pamphlet titled *Why Jews Must Be Resettled from the Industrial Regions of the Country* were found. The Doctors' Plot was the only Stalin purge that was never completed. In 1953, before it could be placed in high gear, Stalin lapsed into a coma, and while he was incapacitated, his assistants recognized the irrationality of the purge. They quashed any further persecutions of anyone associated with the Doctors' Plot.

Between the end of World War II and 1953, while Stalin focused much of his attention on protecting his absolute authority within his nation, he also committed time to crafting a foreign policy that reflected his nation's newly acquired power in the international community. Most of all, Stalin worked to counter what he viewed to be the threat of American capitalism. "How could one expect a lasting peace," Stalin asked, "if capitalism with its imperialism remained?"[59]

Chapter Six

THE COLD WAR AND STALIN'S CONDEMNATION

At the end of World War II, Stalin controlled a burgeoning super-power nation, the most formidable on the European continent. America had also emerged from the war as a superpower touting the world's most robust industry and mightiest military. Unfortunately, the distinctively different and conflicting forms of governments and economies of the two superpowers bred suspicion of the other. Stalin accused the American president Harry Truman of plotting to destroy the Soviet Union in pursuit of world domination, and Truman accused Stalin of plotting to destroy America for the same reason.

Stalin moved decisively to counter the perceived American threat. To confront and contain America, Stalin committed trillions of dollars to rebuilding and enlarging his military, expanding his alliances with other countries, conducting sophisticated propaganda campaigns, and infiltrating America's operations with spies. President Truman engaged in the same provocative behavior, which had the effect of locking the two superpowers in a postwar struggle of nerves, threats, propaganda, and nuclear weapon proliferation. The constant state of anxiety created by this situation was dubbed the Cold War, to distinguish it from a "hot war" of colliding armies.

Stalin quickly consolidated the eight Eastern European countries awarded him at the Potsdam Conference. Mindful of the invasions of the Soviet Union by America in 1917 and then by Germany in 1941, Stalin set the countries up as a buffer zone separating his citizens from the rest of Europe. He also established Communist governments in each one

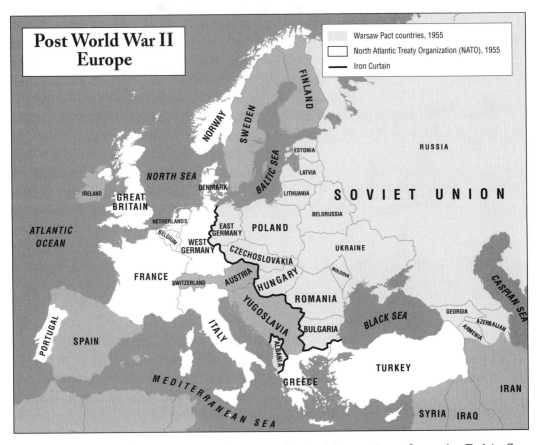

Post World War II Europe

Warsaw Pact countries, 1955
North Atlantic Treaty Organization (NATO), 1955
Iron Curtain

that were under his direct control. From that time forward, these nations became known as Soviet bloc or Soviet satellite nations.

Stalin's Iron Curtain

The Soviet bloc isolated all Soviet citizens from the American threat. Always leery of allowing his citizens to visit Western democracies with higher standards of living, Stalin closed all borders and denied requests for passports. He also ordered the construction of barbed-wire fences and machine-gun posts running along the western boundaries of

Soviet bloc nations from the Baltic Sea to the Adriatic. In 1946, as the impenetrable barrier went up to stem the flow of refugees hoping to escape to better lives, Winston Churchill presented his famous "Iron Curtain" speech at Westminster College in Fulton, Missouri, during which he said:

From Stettin in the Baltic to Trieste in the Adriatic an iron curtain has descended across the Continent. Behind that line lie all the capitals of the ancient states of Central and Eastern Europe. Warsaw, Berlin,

Prague, Vienna, Budapest, Belgrade, Bucharest and Sofia; all these famous cities and the populations around them lie in what I must call the Soviet sphere, and all are subject, in one form or another, not only to Soviet influence but to a very high and in some cases increasing measure of control from Moscow.[60]

In addition to preventing anyone from escaping the Soviet Union, a second function of the Iron Curtain was controlling the flow of people and infor-

mation into it. The free flow of information threatened Stalin's grip on his nation. Fearing ideas and information that might contradict or challenge his party line, Stalin ordered all radio transmissions into the Soviet Union to be jammed and all incoming mail, books, and magazines either confiscated or censored.

Stalin's next step to neutralize American aggression was to develop an atomic bomb. During the Potsdam negotiations, Truman had notified Stalin that America had developed a nuclear

Winston Churchill delivers his "Iron Curtain" speech in which he condemned Stalin's policy of completely isolating the Soviet Union from the West.

Stalin's Quiet Life

Stalin was a tireless worker who regularly worked seven days a week, took few vacations, and shunned an opulent lifestyle in favor of simplicity. Stalin made occasional public speeches and presided over annual Soviet holiday parades, but he preferred to work in the privacy of one of several cabin retreats located within a few hours' drive of Moscow.

Whenever Stalin departed to one of his retreats, he loaded up a box of papers to work on and invited a few close friends, primarily men, to accompany him. During the day, Stalin could be found working at his desk while smoking one of dozens of pipes. He reviewed reports, barked orders to advisers, and dictated letters and memos that would be taken back to Moscow and distributed to key members of his cabinet. At midday he enjoyed a brisk walk in the nearby woods and then returned to his desk for the remainder of the afternoon.

Evening meals at the retreats were large, boisterous affairs. The kitchen staff knew of his voracious appetite and fondness for red meat. They regularly prepared a variety of venison, beef, wild boar, and even bear. Stalin enjoyed consuming several pounds at dinner followed by desserts. Dinner-table conversations covered a variety of topics that wandered from politics to hunting to favorite Russian novelists.

Following dinner, alcohol flowed freely. Although Stalin enjoyed alcohol, he managed to remain more sober than many of his friends. As the evenings wore on, a general drunkenness ensued that could lead to petty personal attacks on political foes but more often led to lewd conversations about women, including wives of party members.

Stalin works outdoors as other members of his family relax during a stay at one of his cabins.

bomb, an announcement that did not seem to startle him. Later that year, however, when American bombers dropped two atomic bombs on Japan, Stalin was forced to hasten the development of his own atomic bomb capability to deter America's ability to attack Soviet cities.

The Nuclear Arms Race

The reason Stalin did not appear startled to hear from Truman about America's nuclear bomb program was that he already knew about it. Unbeknownst to Truman, Stalin had approved of a plan in 1943 to infiltrate top-secret American laboratories engaged in the production of nuclear bombs. As American scientists solved a variety of complex problems controlling and detonating nuclear material, Soviet spies had been smuggling the information back to the Soviet Union.

When America bombed Japan, Stalin accelerated his nation's atomic bomb project by tripling the budget. Stalin's willingness to spare no expense in developing an atomic bomb was made evident in a conversation he had with Igor Kurchatov, the director of the Soviet atomic project: "If a child doesn't cry, the mother doesn't know what he needs. Ask for whatever you like. You won't be refused."[61] Stalin also ordered several top nuclear scientists who had been banished to the gulags to be released to work on the project.

Stalin ordered the construction of a secret city where the atomic bomb would be constructed. Scientists, stockpiles of uranium, and other materials and equipment needed for the construction of the bomb were gathered in a city built by forced labor three hundred miles east of Moscow known as Arzamas-16. On August 29, 1949, the Soviets stunned America and the rest of the world by exploding their first atomic bomb several years before American intelligence officers believed they would have the ability to do so.

The significance of developing the atomic bomb from Stalin's point of view was that it would deter America from striking Soviet cities. The belief that America might attack the Soviet Union was later revealed by one of Stalin's chief scientists, who commented, "If we had been a year or a year and a half later with the atomic bomb, we would surely have felt it on ourselves."[62]

The Soviet development of the atomic bomb escalated Cold War tensions. Several U.S. scientists argued for an all-out effort to build an even more powerful weapon: a hydrogen bomb. Edward Teller, one of America's leading physicists, pushed for a program to build a hydrogen bomb that he called "the Super." In 1951 Teller commented, "If the Russians demonstrate a Super before we possess one, our situation will be hopeless."[63]

Besides confronting America's nuclear capability, Stalin had strategies to confront America's influence in foreign countries around the world. While

America was supporting foreign governments with financial aid and military equipment in exchange for embracing American democracy and capitalism, Stalin was offering similar deals to foreign countries if they would embrace communism.

Spreading Communism

Stalin's next political move was to spread communism around the globe. His motive, as with all his other policies during the Cold War, was to confront America. By the early 1950s, Stalin was making overtures and promises of assistance to other nations willing to embrace the new economic experiment with communism. Stalin focused on nations throughout the world that might be ripe for a revolution.

At the close of the Second World War, a social upheaval in China caught Stalin's attention. A peasants' revolt, similar to the 1917 revolt in Russia, was under way. In 1949 Stalin made overtures to assist the peasant Communist leader Mao Tse-tung with agricultural reforms and an economic plan to create peasant collective farms. Stalin was especially interested in promoting communism in China because of its immense size and population. A successful Communist revolution there, then home to more than half a billion people, might encourage other nations to experiment with communism rather than follow America's example of capitalism. In October 1949 Mao orchestrated a successful Communist revolution.

The success in China inspired Stalin to assist and encourage other Asian nations to embrace and expand communism. In 1950 Stalin encouraged Kim Il Sung, the Communist ruler of North Korea, to invade South Korea. Stalin had assumed that America would not interfere and that Kim would be able to unite the entire Korean peninsula as a Communist state. Stalin's intervention in Korean affairs caused the United Nations to dispatch troops to the war zone and successfully defend South Korea.

Stalin also spent money supporting local Communist parties in dozens of other nations even though he did not expect them to incite revolutions. Nonetheless, even in Western European nations, citizens voted for and elected Communist Party politicians who influenced the politics of England, France, and Italy. They worked to influence international and domestic policies in ways that promoted communism. Communist Party members sought to increase trade with the Soviet Union at the expense of American trade, to restrict the American military presence in their nations, and to teach about communism and the history of Communist countries in public schools.

In the mid-1950s even America experienced a sudden and unanticipated increase in Communist Party activity. Stalin took delight in taunting President Truman when the American Communist Party emerged and proposed politicians for a variety of low-level offices. Al-

In 1949 the Soviet Union detonated its first nuclear bomb at this remote site in Kazakhstan. Soviet development of nuclear technology escalated Cold War tensions.

though American Communist politicians never experienced much success, their presence caused considerable anxiety within America.

Stalin's Death

Stalin's willingness to confront American power strengthened his cult of personality. To millions of Soviet citizens he was a hero. Despite the hard times, the persecutions, and immense suffering, many hailed Stalin as the leader who had elevated their nation to the status of a superpower following their victory over the Germans and then the leader who dared to confront American imperialism. In the streets of Moscow, many citizens felt safer as they hurried to their jobs and to schools knowing that their nation had nuclear bombs and that China was on their side against the Americans.

But on March 5, 1953, Soviets paused when they heard the news that Stalin had died. Stalin suffered a massive stroke on March 1 but, for a variety of reasons, was unattended for four days. The reasons

Chinese Communists march with posters of Stalin. After World War II, Stalin encouraged Communist revolutions in China and other Asian nations.

included Stalin's order that he not be disturbed, difficulties finding a suitable doctor, and delays in gathering together his closest advisers to decide how to handle the delicate situation. Stalin's body was finally washed and transported to the Kremlin mortuary. There, an autopsy was performed. After the autopsy was completed, Stalin's body was given to the embalmers to prepare it for the three days it would be on public display.

The nation was split over Stalin's death. For millions who languished in the gulags and for millions more who had suffered the loss of family and friends due to his tyrannical impulses, Stalin's death was met with jubilation. Yet for millions of others, those untouched by his repression, there was sadness for the loss of the man who had defeated the German invaders and, more recently, had dared to oppose the American threat. This divi-

A Mysterious Death

The four days between Stalin's stroke and the announcement of his death raised questions about how the dictator actually died. Several highly irregular events took place during those four days that have led several leading scholars to speculate that he may have been murdered.

When Stalin retired for the night early on March 1, his chief bodyguard, Viktor Khrustalev, told the others to go to bed. This order was greeted with cheers because Stalin never released his bodyguards because of fears of assassination while he slept. Delighted to retire early, the guards slept late the following morning, as did Stalin. Or so it appeared. The guards began to worry when Stalin had not emerged from his bedroom the next day by 2 P.M. By 10 P.M. they finally entered to check on him.

The guards found Stalin incoherent in his bed and soaked in his own urine. They called his closest comrades but none arrived for an entire day, suggesting to some historians that they were in no hurry to get him to a hospital. One close friend said that he had located a Jewish doctor but knew that Stalin would never allow a Jew to attend to him.

On March 3 a non-Jewish doctor was found to report that Stalin had suffered a severe stroke. Yet the doctor did not rush Stalin to a hospital. The next morning Stalin was pronounced dead. A few historians, especially Edvard Radzinsky, see a plot against Stalin in this questionable chain of events. Radzinsky argues that Stalin was injected with poison by the guard Khrustalev, under the orders of several Communist leaders who for years had hoped for Stalin's death to rid the nation of his unchecked terror.

Stalin's body lies in state in 1953. To this day, the precise circumstances surrounding the dictator's death remain a mystery.

sion of emotion within the Soviet Union was witnessed by Stalin biographer Leonida Krushelnycky, who remembered, "Many openly wept for the man they called 'Father' and 'Teacher.' Others in prison camps across the land allowed themselves to exchange secret smiles and hope that things would be different now."[64]

Stalin's body was temporarily displayed in the Hall of Columns, where thousands of people lined up in the snow to see it. The crowds were so dense that some people were trampled and others crushed against cars and traffic barriers. Hundreds of people died trying to get a glimpse of the leader's corpse. On March 9 Stalin's coffin was carried from the Hall of Columns to Lenin's tomb in Moscow's Red Square for interment next to Lenin. At the entry to the great red granite tomb, Stalin's name was etched just below Lenin's.

Svetlana was the only family member to attend her father's funeral. She had always been his favorite child, which is reflected in the many tender letters they wrote each other. As a young woman after her mother's suicide, she had delighted in serving as the family hostess for social affairs at their Moscow home, but she never engaged in politics. For many years, the two seemed to enjoy a happy father-daughter relationship. As Svetlana matured, however, she became distraught over her father's callous nature and gradually withdrew from his world of oppressive suspicion and vindictive behavior. Svetlana agreed to attend her father's elaborate state funeral but refused to kiss his forehead, as was expected of her.

De-Stalinization

Stalin had presented himself as the father of all Soviets, a wise leader, and the continuer of Lenin's cause for worldwide Communist revolution, but many knew otherwise. Shortly after Stalin's death, people who knew and feared him felt confident that the time had arrived to acknowledge openly and without recrimination the truth—that Stalin had been responsible for the deaths of millions of their own countrymen and the ruthless subjugation of millions more.

Nikita Khrushchev emerged as Stalin's successor. He had worked for Stalin and had firsthand knowledge of the dictator's cruelty. Khrushchev took the initiative to publicly expose Stalin's terror. He understood that some citizens knew about isolated events of cruelty and murder, but few knew about all of it. Khrushchev became the person most responsible for destroying Stalin's cult of personality and myth of the "great leader" by spearheading a movement to eradicate the false memory of Stalin. In a speech to the closed session of the Communist Party in 1956, Khrushchev shocked his listeners by denouncing Stalin's dictatorial rule. He also attacked the crimes committed by Stalin's closest associates.

One of Khrushchev's criticisms of Stalin was his use of fear to control people. The fear of possible death or deportation for speaking out against Stalin's policies caused people to remain silent even when they disagreed with him. This fear that so often silenced people was once demonstrated by Khrushchev. In the course of denouncing Stalin one day, Khrushchev was interrupted by a voice from the audience: "You were one of Stalin's colleagues, why didn't you stop him?" "Who said that!?" Khrushchev roared. The room was quickly filled with an agonizing silence finally broken by Khrushchev himself. "Now," he remarked in a quiet voice, "you know why."[65]

Khrushchev's efforts became known as "de-Stalinization," the process of neutralizing Stalin's influence by exposing the full extent of his terror, reversing many of his destructive policies, removing monuments dedicated to him, and renaming Stalingrad Volgograd. Khrushchev reversed much of Stalin's worst excesses by restoring some legal procedures, reducing the power of the NKVD, closing many of the gulags, and sending fewer political prisoners to those that remained open. This new atmosphere of greater freedom was a considerable improvement from the days of Stalin.

In 1958 the decision was made to remove Stalin from his place of honor next to Lenin. At the Twenty-second Party Congress, an old, devoted Bolshevik woman, Dora Abramovna Lazurkina, stood up and voiced the sentiment of millions:

My heart is always full of Lenin. Comrades, I could survive the most difficult moments only because I carried Lenin in my heart, and always consulted him on what to do. Yesterday I consulted him. He was standing there before me as if he were alive, and he said: "It is unpleasant to be next to Stalin, who did so much harm to the party."[66]

Khrushchev followed by reading a decree ordering the removal of Stalin's remains:

The further retention in the mausoleum of the sarcophagus with the bier of J.V. Stalin shall be recognized as inappropriate since the serious violations by Stalin of Lenin's precepts, abuse of power, mass repressions against honorable Soviet people, and other activities in the period of the personality cult make it impossible to leave the bier with his body in the mausoleum of V.I. Lenin.[67]

A few days later, Stalin's body was quietly removed from the tomb and his name obliterated from the entrance. There were no ceremonies and no fanfare. Stalin's body was buried near minor leaders of the Russian Revolution.

Stalin's successor Nikita Khrushchev denounces the former dictator in a 1956 speech. Khruschev worked to reverse many of Stalin's most brutal excesses.

Stalin's Image Today

As the twenty-first century pushes forward, Stalin is widely vilified by most contemporary historians as the butcher of millions of his own people. No newly released documentation is likely to change that perception.

A variety of historians and political leaders have recently commented on Stalin's historical legacy. Mikhail Gorbachev, the president of the Soviet Union until 1991, steered a moderate position noting what he perceived to be a duality in Stalin's personality that was both constructive and destructive:

We must see both Stalin's indisputable contribution to the struggle for socialism and the defense of its gains and the flagrant political mistakes and the arbitrary actions committed by him and his entourage, for which our people paid a great price and which had grave consequences for the life of our society.[68]

Historian Ross Douthat is not as generous as Gorbachev. After a lengthy discussion of Stalin's life and political career, Douthat concludes his history with a condemnation of the Soviet leader:

Stalin and His Son Yakov

Stalin's well-documented cruelty manifested in a variety of ways during the Great Terror and again following the Second World War. Although he was directly responsible for the deaths of tens of millions of Soviets, one death in particular that he caused stands out as profoundly wicked: that of his son Yakov.

Yakov was the oldest and Stalin's least favorite of his three children. Sent away when he was a baby to live with relatives, Yakov did not become acquainted with his father until he was a teenager. The distant relationship resulted in a mutual dislike for each other, and when Yakov matured, the animosity between the two was pronounced. Despite Yakov's lofty status as Stalin's son, he accomplished little, and when the Second World War broke out, Stalin sent Yakov to the western front as a common foot soldier to stop the German advance.

In 1943 Yakov was captured by the Germans. As soon as they realized who they had captured, the German high command offered to trade him for one of their generals, Friedrich Paulus, who was a prisoner of war in Russia. Unfortunately for Yakov, when the

offer was reported to Stalin, his father refused the trade commenting that trading a general for a foot soldier was not a fair exchange. Furthermore, Stalin added, prisoners of war were cowardly traitors. Failing to effect a trade, the Germans executed Yakov.

Nazi officials interrogate Stalin's son Yakov in 1943.

He was a destructive force, perhaps the most destructive human being of this long and bloody century—more destructive even than his great rival, Hitler, whose own regime went down under the boots of the Red [Soviet] Army. He was a political genius with the soul of a sadistic thug, a paranoid and cruel man with his hands on the reins of a great nation; the shadow that he casts, even today, is long and dark and full of terrors.[69]

Even some contemporary Marxists have difficulty complimenting Stalin. In 2003 Alan Woods, a Marxist historian and political theorist writing for Marxist publications, described Stalin as a man who was willing to sacrifice his nation for his own ideological pursuits. Woods

Although this museum in Gori honors Stalin, many Russians today condemn the Soviet leader as an evil dictator who brutalized an entire nation.

believes that Stalin's rule was reckless and driven by self-serving motives:

> Who could seriously maintain now that Stalin had some idea of a general order of things? Or that he had some ideology? Stalin never had any ideology or conviction or ideas or principles. Stalin always held whatever opinions made it easy for him to tyrannize others, to keep them in fear and guilt. Today the teacher and leader may say one thing, tomorrow something else. He never cared what he said, as long as he held onto his power.[70]

NOTES

Introduction:
Joseph Stalin: The Enigma

1. Nikolai Tolstoy, *Stalin's Secret War*. New York: Holt, Rinehart & Winston, 1981, p. 34.
2. Quoted in *BBC News*, "What Do You Know About Winnie?" 2002. http://news.bbc.co.uk/1/hi/uk/25110 79.stm.
3. Bertram Wolfe, *Three Who Made a Revolution: A Biographical History of Lenin, Trotsky, and Stalin*. New York: Cooper Square, 1948, p. 405.
4. Edvard Radzinsky, *Stalin*, trans. H.T. Willets. New York: Sceptre, 1996, pp. 4–5.

Chapter 1:
Modest Beginnings

5. Ronald Hingley, *Joseph Stalin: Man and Legend*. New York: McGraw-Hill, 1974, p. 2.
6. Quoted in Radzinsky, *Stalin*, p. 31.
7. Quoted in Helen Rappaport, *Joseph Stalin: A Biographical Companion*. Santa Barbara, CA: ABC-CLIO, 1999, p. 272.
8. Hingley, *Joseph Stalin*, p. 5.
9. Quoted in Hingley, *Joseph Stalin*, p. 11.
10. Quoted in Hingley, *Joseph Stalin*, p. 15.
11. Spartacus Educational, "Joseph Stalin," 2003. www.spartacus.school net.co.uk/RUSstalin.htm.

12. Quoted in Wolfe, *Three Who Made a Revolution*, p. 422.
13. Quoted in Wolfe, *Three Who Made a Revolution*, p. 425.

Chapter 2:
Stepping-Stones to Power

14. Christopher Read, *The Stalin Years*. New York: Palgrave Macmillan, 2003, p. 1.
15. Joseph Stalin, "Lenin," *Pravda*, February 12, 1924. www.socialnerve.org/lenin/len/other/stalin3.html.
16. Quoted in Wolfe, *Three Who Made a Revolution*, p. 460.
17. Quoted in Philip Pomper, *Lenin, Trotsky, and Stalin: The Intelligentsia and Power*. New York: Columbia University Press, 1990, p. 177.
18. Quoted in Albert Marrin, *Stalin: Russia's Man of Steel*. New York: Penguin, 1993, p. 28.
19. Wolfe, *Three Who Made a Revolution*, p. 89.
20. Quoted in Wolfe, *Three Who Made a Revolution*, p. 562.
21. Pomper, *Lenin, Trotsky, and Stalin*, p. 176.
22. Quoted in Hingley, *Joseph Stalin*, p. 75.
23. Pomper, *Lenin, Trotsky, and Stalin*, p. 258.
24. Quoted in Spartacus Educational, "Joseph Stalin."

25. Quoted in Robert Conquest, *The Great Terror: Stalin's Purge of the Thirties.* New York: Collier, 1973, p. 114.

26. Quoted in Miklós Kun, *Stalin: An Unknown Portrait.* Budapest: Central European University Press, 2003, p. 179.

27. Pomper, *Lenin, Trotsky, and Stalin*, p. 258.

28. Quoted in Conquest, *The Great Terror*, pp. 714–15.

Chapter 3: The Great Terror

29. Quoted in Conquest, *The Great Terror*, p. 43.

30. Quoted in Library of Congress, "Ukrainian Famine," 1996. www.loc.gov/exhibits/archives/ukra. html.

31. Hingley, *Joseph Stalin*, p. 204.

32. Read, *The Stalin Years*, p. 107.

33. Robert C. Tucker, *Stalin in Power: The Revolution from Above, 1928–1941.* New York: W.W. Norton, 1990, p. 274.

34. Quoted in Spartacus Educational, "Joseph Stalin."

35. Quoted in Steven Kreis, "The Age of Totalitarianism: Stalin and Hitler," *History Guide*, 2000. www.historyguide.org/europe/lecture10.html.

36. Kreis, "The Age of Totalitarianism."

37. Rappaport, *Joseph Stalin*, p. 194.

38. Quoted in Rappaport, *Joseph Stalin*, p. 114.

39. Quoted in Read, *The Stalin Years*, p. 128.

Chapter 4: The Second World War

40. Quoted in Hingley, *Joseph Stalin*, p. 294.

41. Quoted in Radzinsky, *Stalin*, p. 452.

42. Quoted in Ludmil Kostadinov, "The Role of Stalin and of the Communist Party in the Great Patriotic War," Solidaire, 2003. www.ptb.be/scripts/article.phtml?obid=19969&lang=3&bNoStat=1.

43. Hingley, *Joseph Stalin*, p. 318.

44. Quoted in Helen Rappaport, *Joseph Stalin: A Biographical Companion.* Santa Barbara, CA: ABC-CLIO, p. 131

45. Adam Ulam, *Stalin: The Man and His Era.* Boston: Beacon Press, 1989, p. 599.

46. Quoted in Kun, *Stalin*, p. 326.

47. Quoted in Hingley, *Joseph Stalin*, p. 365.

48. Quoted in Hingley, *Joseph Stalin*, p. 365.

Chapter 5: The Terror Returns

49. Quoted in Ulam, *Stalin*, p. 615.

50. Aleksandr Solzhenitsyn, *The Gulag Archipelago: 1918–1956*, trans. Thomas Whitney and Harry Willetts. New York: Harper & Row, 1985, p. 238.

51. Hingley, *Joseph Stalin*, p. 372.

52. Ulam, *Stalin*, p. 634.

53. Quoted in Radzinsky, *Stalin*, p. 503.

54. Hingley, *Joseph Stalin*, p. 372.

55. Quoted in Radzinsky, *Stalin*, p. 519.

56. Quoted in H. Schonberg, "Dimitri Shostakovich," University of Chicago, http://home.uchicago.edu/~nat222/viktor/shostakovich.html.

57. Schonberg, "Dimitri Shostakovich."
58. Quoted in Hingley, *Joseph Stalin*, p. 415.
59. Quoted in Ulam, *Stalin*, p. 630.

Chapter 6: The Cold War and Stalin's Condemnation

60. Quoted in Paul Halsall, "Winston S. Churchill: 'Iron Curtain Speech,' March 5, 1946," Modern History Sourcebook, 1997. www.fordham.edu/halsall/mod/churchill-iron.html.
61. Quoted in Rappaport, *Joseph Stalin*, p. 12.
62. Quoted in Rappaport, *Joseph Stalin*, p. 12.
63. Quoted in PBS, "Race for the Superbomb," 1999. www.pbs.org/wgbh/amex/bomb.
64. Leonida Krushelnycky, "The Mystery of Stalin's Death," *BBC News*, 2003. http://news.bbc.co.uk/2/hi/europe/2793501.stm.
65. Quoted in Anecdotage, "Stalin," www.anecdotage.com/index.php?aid=11286.
66. Quoted in Jennifer Rosenberg, "Stalin's Body Removed from Lenin's Tomb," 20th Century History, 2003. http://history1900s.about.com/library/weekly/aa040600a.htm.
67. Quoted in Rosenberg, "Stalin's Body Removed from Lenin's Tomb."
68. Quoted in Jonathan Lewis and Phillip Whitehead, *Stalin: A Time for Judgment.* London: Methuen, 1990, p. 1.
69. Ross Douthat, "Joseph Stalin," *Spark Notes,* www.sparknotes.com/biography/Stalin/sectionII.rhtml.
70. Alan Woods, "Fifty Years After the Death of the Tyrant Stalin and the Intellectuals," *In Defence of Marxism*, 2003. www.marxist.com/History/Stalin_death4.html.

For Further Reading

Books

W.G. Kravitsky, *In Stalin's Secret Service: Memoirs of the First Soviet Master Spy to Defect*. New York: Enigma, 2000. This is the true story of a man who worked as a spy for Stalin and later defected to America. Kravitsky presents a spellbinding memoir of espionage and intrigue while he worked for the NKVD.

Albert Marrin, *Stalin: Russia's Man of Steel*. New York: Penguin, 1993. Marrin's book is a very readable account of the life of the man who shaped the Soviet Union from pre-revolutionary Russia to its evolution as a superpower. Includes a handful of valuable black-and-white photographs.

Christopher Read, *The Stalin Years*. New York: Palgrave Macmillan, 2003. This book contains a collection of articles written by historians that focus on a variety of themes during Stalin's reign.

Harrison Salisbury, *900 Days: The Siege of Leningrad*. New York: Macmillan, 2000. Salisbury tells the dramatic story of the nine-hundred-day siege of Leningrad by the Germans.

Simon Sebag-Montefiore, *Stalin: The Court of the Red Tsar*. New York: Knopf, 2003. This history of Stalin is a very readable book for young adults that highlights key personalities in Stalin's life from his birth to his death.

Aleksandr Solzhenitsyn, *The Gulag Archipelago: 1918–1956*. Trans. Thomas Whitney and Harry Willetts. New York: Harper & Row, 1985. This Nobel Prize–winning novel, originally published in 1973, is an exhaustive and compelling account of life in a gulag based on Solzhenitsyn's own eight-year experience.

Robert C. Tucker, *Stalin in Power: The Revolution from Above, 1928–1941*. New York: W.W. Norton, 1990. This book is widely acclaimed as one of the great works on Stalin. The author's narrative style makes the book a pleasurable read.

Web Sites

BBC News (http://news.bbc.co.uk). The British Broadcasting Corporation (BBC), England's most well known news organization, reports events from around the world. Each day this Web site offers a handful of selected news articles in abbreviated form.

Modern History Sourcebook (www.ford ham.edu/halsall/mod/modsbook.html). Fordham University provides an electronic sourcebook of primary-source material covering an array of political, social, and economic topics. Each selection is chosen to illustrate a particular important event or person.

Public Broadcasting Service (www.pbs. org). PBS provides a wide variety of television programs highlighted on this Web site. Programs include discussions and photographs of many historical figures and events, including those of the Soviet Union.

20th Century History (http://history 1900s.about.com). This is a site geared toward the young adult audience that provides thousands of topics about the twentieth century. Most discuss serious historical events, but others entertain the reader with stories about fads, foods, and famous celebrities.

WORKS CONSULTED

Books

Robert Conquest, *The Great Terror: Stalin's Purge of the Thirties.* New York: Collier, 1973. This book is widely accepted as the definitive work on Stalin's Great Terror. It is a well-documented portrayal of the death of millions in Stalin's peacetime consolidation of power.

Robin Edmonds, *The Big Three: Churchill, Roosevelt, and Stalin in Peace and War.* London: Hamish Hamilton, 1991. This highly acclaimed book discusses the summit meetings at Yalta and Potsdam toward the end of World War II. The book also presents fascinating insights into the personalities and relationships of Churchill, Roosevelt, and Stalin.

J. Arch Getty and Roberta T. Manning, *Stalinist Terror: New Perspectives.* Cambridge, England: Cambridge University Press, 1993. This work is a compilation of several individual studies documenting the period of the Great Terror between 1932 and 1938.

Ronald Hingley, *Joseph Stalin: Man and Legend.* New York: McGraw-Hill, 1974. Of the numerous biographies about Stalin, Hingley's is one of the most objective and comprehensive. The author thoroughly covers Stalin's life from birth to death, with particular emphasis on the 1930s and 1940s.

Miklós Kun, *Stalin: An Unknown Portrait.* Budapest: Central European University Press, 2003. In addition to much commonly reported information about Stalin, Kun adds significant insight into Stalin's relationships with his family and close advisers.

Jonathan Lewis and Phillip Whitehead, *Stalin: A Time for Judgment.* London: Methuen, 1990. The authors discuss Stalin's transformation of agriculture and reconstruction of industry in detail. They focus on forced collectivization, the impact of the great famine, and forced labor camps.

Karl Marx and Friedrich Engels, *The Communist Manifesto.* Oxford, England: Oxford University Press, 1992. First published in 1848 when Marx was twenty-nine years old, this book is considered by historians to be one of the most revolutionary books of the last two centuries. Considered the "bible" for all communist revolutions, the book lays out Marx's philosophy for revolutions to distribute equitably all capital among all workers.

Philip Pomper, *Lenin, Trotsky, and Stalin: The Intelligentsia and Power.* New York: Columbia University Press, 1990. This work focuses on the three leaders of the Bolshevik revolution from the late 1880s to Lenin's death, Trotsky's decline, and Stalin's rise to power. Pomper sheds valuable light on the relationships among the three men.

Edvard Radzinsky, *Stalin.* Trans. H.T. Willets. New York: Sceptre, 1996. The author was granted privileged access to Russia's secret archives in 1992 and based on them he wrote the first in-depth biography containing that new information.

Helen Rappaport, *Joseph Stalin: A Biographical Companion.* Santa Barbara, CA: ABC-CLIO, 1999. This is an excellent book written in dictionary form that highlights all of the major events and people in Stalin's life. Most entries are two to three pages.

Nikolai Tolstoy, *Stalin's Secret War.* New York: Holt, Rinehart & Winston, 1981. This book covers Stalin from his prewar to postwar management of the Soviet Union.

Adam Ulam, *Stalin: The Man and His Era.* Boston: Beacon Press, 1989. Ulam's excellent biography puts into perspective how Stalin rose to absolute power over the Soviet Union. Ulam portrays Stalin as an extremely intelligent politician who effectively suppressed the Russian intelligentsia.

Dmitri Volkogonov, *Stalin: Triumph and Tragedy.* Trans. Harold Shukman. New York: Grove, 1991. A comprehensive biography of Stalin from a Marxist-Leninist perspective of the Russian Revolution.

Bertram Wolfe, *Three Who Made a Revolution: A Biographical History of Lenin, Trotsky, and Stalin.* New York: Cooper Square, 1948. This monumental triple biography weaves together the personal and public lives of the triumvirate behind the 1917 Russian Revolution.

Internet Sources

Anecdotage, "Stalin," www.anecdotage. com/index.php?aid/11286.

BBC News, "What Do You Know About Winnie?" 2002. http://news.bbc.co. uk./1/hi/uk/2511079.stm.

Dictators and Tyrants Database, "Joseph Stalin," 2003. http://dictatorstyrants. bravepages.com.

Ross Douthat, "Joseph Stalin," *Spark Notes,* www.sparknotes.com/biogra phy/Stalin/sectionII.rhtml.

Paul Halsall, "Winston S. Churchill: 'Iron Curtain Speech,' March 5, 1946," Modern History Sourcebook, 1997. www.fordham.edu/halsall/mod/chur chill-iron.html.

Bruce Harris, "Joseph Stalin," Moreorless, 2002. www.moreorless.au.com/killers/stalin.htm.

Ludmil Kostadinov, "The Role of Stalin and of the Communist Party in the Great Patriotic War," Solidaire, 2003. www.ptb.bescripts/article.phtml?obid=19969&lang=3&bNoStat=1.

Steven Kreis, "The Age of Totalitarianism: Stalin and Hitler," *History Guide*, 2000. www.historyguide.org/europe/lecture10.html.

Leonida Krushelnycky, "The Mystery of Stalin's Death," *BBC News*, 2003. http://news.bbc.co.uk2/hi/europe/2793501.stm.

Library of Congress, "Ukrainian Famine," 1996. www.loc.gov/exhibits/archives/ukra.html.

Charles Lutton, "Stalin's War: Victims and Accomplices," Historical Revisionism, 2003. www.vho.org/GB/Journals/JHR/5/1/Lutton84-94.html

Marxists Internet Archive, V.I. Lenin, "A Letter to J.V. Stalin," December 6, 1912, www.marxists.org/archive/lenin/works/1912/dec/11.htm.

PBS, "Race for the Superbomb," 1999. www.pbs.org/wgbh/amex/bomb.

Vadim Z. Rogovin, *1937: Stalin's Year of Terror*, World Socialist Web Site 2004. www.wsws.org/exhibits/1937/title.htm.

Jennifer Rosenberg, "Stalin's Body Removed from Lenin's Tomb," 20th Century History, 2003. http://history1900s.about.com/library/weekly/aa040600a.htm.

H. Schonberg, "Dimitri Shostakovich," University of Chicago, http://home.uchicago.edu/~nat222/viktor/shostakovish.html.

Spartacus Educational, "Joseph Stalin," 2003. www.spartacus.schoolnet.co.uk/RUSstalin.htm.

Joseph Stalin, "Lenin," *Pravda*, February 12, 1924. www.socialnerve.org/lenin/len/other/stalin3.html.

Alan Woods, "Fifty Years After the Death of the Tyrant Stalin and the Intellectuals," *In Defence of Marxism*, 2003. www.marxist.com/History/Stalin_death4.html.

INDEX

PICTURE CREDITS

ABOUT THE AUTHOR

James Barter received his undergraduate degree in history and classics at the University of California at Berkeley, followed by his graduate degree in ancient history and archaeology at the University of Pennsylvania. Mr. Barter has taught history as well as Latin and Greek.

A Fulbright scholar at the American Academy in Rome, Mr. Barter worked on archaeological sites in and around the city as well as Etruscan sites north of Rome and Roman sites in the Naples area. Mr. Barter also has worked and traveled extensively in Greece.

Mr. Barter resides in Rancho Santa Fe, California, and lectures throughout the San Diego area.